I BECAME THE
Boat People

A REFUGEE'S PATH TO AMERICA

DON LAO, CPCU

abbott press®
A DIVISION OF WRITER'S DIGEST

Abbott Press books may be ordered through booksellers or by contacting:

Abbott Press
1663 Liberty Drive
Bloomington, IN 47403
www.abbottpress.com
Phone: 1-866-697-5310

Because of the dynamic nature of the Internet, any web addresses or links contained in this book may have changed since publication and may no longer be valid. The views expressed in this work are solely those of the author and do not necessarily reflect the views of the publisher, and the publisher hereby disclaims any responsibility for them.

Any people depicted in stock imagery provided by Thinkstock are models, and such images are being used for illustrative purposes only.
Certain stock imagery © Thinkstock.

ISBN: 978-1-4582-1307-5 (sc)
ISBN: 978-1-4582-1308-2 (hc)
ISBN: 978-1-4582-1306-8 (e)

Library of Congress Control Number: 2013921810

Printed in the United States of America.

Abbott Press rev. date: 12/11/2013

Contents

Preface

This is a depiction of the challenging lives of immigrants who had to endure adversities and overcome many obstacles in order to survive and provide better lives for their loved ones.

This story provides a glimpse of the tenacity and resiliency of people living through three decades of the Vietnam War from the French domination in 1954 to the fall of Saigon in 1975, as well as their journey to a new country as refugees. They were known as The Boat People.

Their struggles included adapting to a completely new culture, learning a new language, competing for jobs in a foreign environment, and coping with ethnic tension. Developing a sense of belonging paled in comparison to the difficultly of uprooting their family to resettle in a new country.

This true story is living proof that a successful and meaningful life can be achieved through the love and support of family, good education, relentless pursuit of goals, diligence, and hard work.

Map of Vietnam

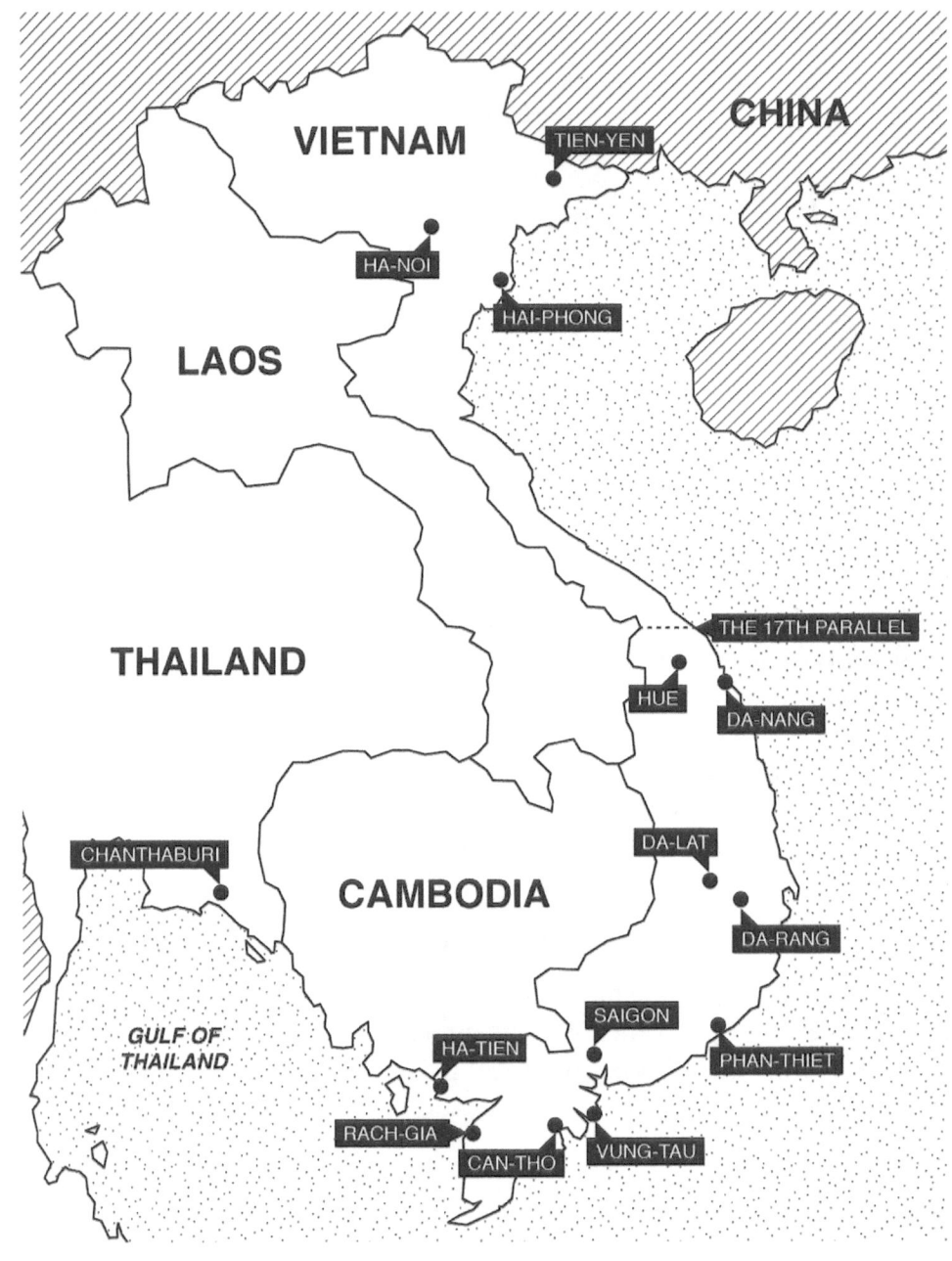

$\mathcal{C}$hapter 1

Moving to Vietnam

The Japanese dominated Vietnam, along with other Southeast Asia countries during WWII. When the Japanese surrendered in 1945, the French took over the domination of Vietnam in 1946.

My Grandpa expanded his business, of a retail store selling imported products in Quangdong (Canton), China, to become an exclusive supplier for the French government and provide transportation services to the French troops in North Vietnam. Grandpa and his first wife had a son and a daughter; he married my Grandma after his first wife passed away. Grandma gave birth to four boys (my Dad, Uncle Chin, Uncle Wing and Uncle Wah) and two girls, Aunt Guy and Aunt Le-Quan.

In order to meet the demand of the expanded business, Grandpa moved his entire family from China to a city called Tien-Yen in North Vietnam during the early 1940's, and I was born there on July 4th, 1948. Everyone lived with Grandpa and Grandma in a multi-room mansion in Tien-Yen.

Tien-Yen was a small town near Mong-Cai, a Vietnamese city bordering China where people crossed between China and Vietnam; it's about 300 kilometers northeast of Ha-Noi, the capital of Vietnam. Tien-Yen's population was about 5,000 and the vast majority of the people there were immigrants from China.

Tien-Yen has a mild climate and beautiful scenery, with rolling hills and a river running through town. Farming was the main occupation because of the fertile soil and favorable climate with abundant rainfall. Fruit trees were also productive; my Mom said grapefruits from the trees in our backyard were especially sweet and juicy. Residents of Tien-Yen were typical country folk who were friendly and cared for one another in this close-knit community with virtually no crimes. The transition for our family was quite smooth with Grandpa's presence and leadership well accepted by the people of Tien-Yen. In fact, we consider Tien-Yen our hometown.

Grandpa was a typical "China-man" – 5'6", 140 pounds with light skin, black hair and brown eyes; we all have a receding front hairline like him. Grandpa went to schools in China and he was multi-lingual, speaking fluent Vietnamese and French in addition to Chinese. He built a good relationship with the French officials and he had high standards in running his business. His honesty and integrity earned the trust and respect of the French as well as his business associates, and the people of Tien-Yen. High-ranking French officials stationed in Tien-Yen were good friends of Grandpa; they visited him frequently and were treated with good food and French wine. Banquets were also held from time to time to entertain these important guests.

In addition to providing the French troops with daily goods and food, our family also owned a fleet of trucks handling their transportation needs, including hauling military supplies for them. Our trucks were often ambushed by the Viet-Minh (the Vietnamese guerilla force) but we were undeterred, with strong support and handsome compensation, from the French government. Dad often told the story of one specific incident where the road in front of our convoy escorted by armored French military vehicle was cut off by the Viet-Minh – later referred to as Viet-Cong (Vietnamese Communists – VC). Our drivers were trapped inside their trucks with some of their tires blown out by the gunfire; they were later rescued by French troops, and Dad brought mechanics to make on-site repairs before the convoy could continue and proceed to their destination.

Grandpa's supplies were transported from the port city of Hai-Phong by cargo boats; they arrived monthly, and laborers were hired to unload the cargo for us. The main items were French wines, cheeses, produce, imported cookies and canned food; these were stacked in a warehouse behind Grandpa's store. A group of women was hired to handle the produce, including peeling of potatoes, to prepare food for the French troops. The storefront catered to local shoppers, but the bulk of our business was focused on meeting the needs of the French.

Grandpa was the largest employer of the town and later became the mayor of Tien-Yen. There were not too many Vietnamese in our town, and we did not sense any resentment with the Chinese running the town thanks to Grandpa's equal employment policy and open-mindedness. Many of his employees, including a few of our truck drivers, were hardworking Vietnamese. Grandpa undoubtedly had everyone's respect and admiration.

Grandpa's son and daughter from his first marriage moved away before I was born, so I don't really know much about them. My Dad was Grandpa's right-hand man; he was heavily involved in running the family business after graduating from high school. Although he was a little taller (5'8"), Dad shared the thin and tall physique like Grandpa, and yes, including the receding hairline in front.

Dad's name is Alan. He became a smoker from entertaining the customers and business associates. He did not drink hard liquor, but he enjoyed beer, and he liked eating roasted peanuts when he had his beer. He played volleyball in his youth. Dad said he also used to play accordion, but he devoted his life to his family and did not have a chance to continue any of his hobbies after we left Tien-Yen. Dad was kind, caring and affectionate, especially with Mom, to whom we had never seen him raise his voice. I had never seen him get into an argument with anyone in his entire life. Some might consider him weak, but his courage was unparalleled when it involved protecting his family.

Dad's duties included overseeing the fleet of trucks, as well as their maintenance and repair. We had our own repair shop, which was staffed with mechanics to perform routine maintenance and on-site repairs, as well as roadside rescue work. Dad kept a supply of spared parts that were often needed for the upkeep of the trucks; orders of the spare parts and new tires often came in with merchandise Grandpa shipped in from the port city of Hai-Phong.

During a stormy night, one of the cargo boats sank. One of the passengers was Aunt Guy coming back from a trip to Hai-Phong. There were no lifeboats so she tied her suitcase to one of her feet and swam ashore unharmed! She was such a good swimmer! Most of the merchandise was lost but there were no casualties.

Aunt Guy was athletic but temperamental; she would fight for anything she wanted to have, and succeeded most of the time. She married a scholar in Tien-Yen, and they had a son, my cousin Khang, a year later.

Dad's younger siblings enjoyed the luxury of good schooling and pampering of the servants, while Grandpa and Dad were busy running the business. My Grandma was the decision maker in all our family matters. Unfortunately, she passed away shortly after I was born. Mom said Grandma died of lung disease that she had for a long time.

The Wedding

Mom and Dad's marriage followed the traditional Chinese custom where a third party acted as middleman in making a proposal to the bride's family. My parents didn't meet until their wedding day, although Dad told me he spotted mom on several occasions in town and was drawn to her beauty. Mom came from a well-respected family; Mom's dad was a well-educated man. He passed away before I was born.

As with all the girls back then, Mom only went to grade school for a few years. Mom was a very pretty lady when she was young. She had shiny black hair, which looked especially beautiful when permed. Mom did not wear makeup very often because she seldom went out; we forgot how beautiful she was until she had a glamour shot makeover on her 50th birthday. She is now in her late 80's and people still say how good she looks when she is garbed in the traditional Chinese gown.

After an acceptance ceremony, which included a lot of gifts, cakes, and lucky money for the bride's family, both sides agreed on a date for the wedding. The Chinese wedding ceremony includes the groom and bride kneeling and serving tea to their grandparents/parents, who would then give well wishes and lucky money sealed inside a red envelope. Both Mom and Dad dressed in traditional Chinese gowns made of colorful red fabrics that symbolize good luck and happiness.

A large dinner party was held for more than 300 guests from both families. There were no restaurants or catering in Tien-Yen for a party this size, so cooks and servers were hired to prepare food based on a pre-determined menu designed by the groom's family. A section of the street leading to our house was closed down to set up tents for dinner tables. Mom said it was a festive and happy day with red banners hung along the street for good luck, and well wishes written on them.

Their first child, Chi, was born a year before me. She and I were extremely competitive, the way bothers and sisters are – always trying to outdo each other, including the attempts to get out of doing unpleasant chores like cleaning the toilet or handling the trash. However, I have to admit Chi always had the upper hand because she is the smarter one – I often ended up doing those unpleasant chores while she was "coincidentally" busy helping Mom with something else!

Mom gave birth to my younger sister (Kum) when I was two years old. Both girls were adorable, with big brown eyes and light skin, but Chi was more active and outgoing. Kum was shy and didn't talk much, but she was very pretty with silky long black hair.

Mom also adopted a girl from an orphanage. Mom named her Ping; she was six years older than Chi. It was a tradition then for well-off couples to adopt a girl as their life-long servant, but Mom did not have the intention to treat Ping that way. Although my Mom did not ask her to work, Ping helped out the group of women with peeling potatoes and cleaning vegetables for food preparation during the day.

Mom said I was an adorable, healthy baby. As boys were seen as heir to the family, I received better attention than my sisters. I was shy and quiet, but I evolved and grew to also be very competitive, a perfectionist, and an overachiever. I have high standards for myself, and I set goals to challenge myself at every stage of my life.

I've been, however, skinny all my life (5'8" and 145 pounds with black hair and brown eyes) except while I was in the military. I was at least 30 pounds heavier during my two years in the military service in the early 1970's.

My sisters and I were well cared for by a military doctor from France with routine physical and dental exams; he made house calls when we were not feeling well. Mom said I had severe rash when I was two years old and she followed the French doctor's instruction to bathe me with French perfume for six months until I was completely cured.

Grandpa's store was well stocked with imported goods from France, so French food was quite familiar to me. The oval-shaped canned pate, freshly baked baguettes and *Vicci* natural spring water were deeply ingrained in me (still my favorites). Soy sauce was substituted with *Maggi* – a popular French seasoning sauce (another favorite of mine). I had all kinds of toys brought by friends of Grandpa. In addition to Mom staying at home, we also had a nanny who took care of us. Mom sometimes took us to Grandpa's store where we would be allowed to have imported cookies and drink bottled spring water from France.

I had many friends from the neighborhood because of Grandpa's status, but my best friend is Khang, one of my cousins. We were the same age and grew up together; Khang often came over and we played with my toys. Khang is now operating a Chinese fast-food restaurant in Long Beach, California, with his wife. He and I are alike, skinny and tall, but his demeanor, hairstyle and the way he talks remind me of Bruce

Lee. Khang laughs a lot and when he does we can hardly see his little bitty eyes.

Moving to Ha-Noi

Although the VC were poorly organized, they won a major battle at Dien-Bien-Phu 300 Kilometers north of Ha-Noi, which started on March 13th, 1954. After two months of intensive fighting, 10,000 French troops surrendered to General Giap of the VC on May 7th, 1954, which marked the beginning of the end of the French domination. It led to the Geneva agreements of 1954 endorsed by the People's Republic of China and signed by all parties involved – France, North Vietnam and South Vietnam.

Major provisions of the agreement include[1]:

1. Designation of the 17th parallel as the DMZ (Demilitarized Zone) separating the North for the communist party, supported by Russia and China, and South Vietnam, backed by the west;
2. Citizens from both sides had the right to choose to reside in either the North or the South within a window of 300 days;
3. Existing French properties and establishments had to be preserved;
4. France would handover the ruling power to Vietnam on September 7th, 1954;
5. Withdrawal of all French troops was to be completed by April of 1956.

When the French troops began to retreat, Grandpa sold off his business in Tien-Yen and moved to Ha-Noi, keeping only a fleet of trucks to continue his contract with the French government. Although our family had no political affiliations, our impeccable business relationship with the French was too precious to lose. It was difficult to see the vanishing

---

[1]   The Book "History of Vietnamese-Chinese" by Mr. Lieu Nguyen

business opportunity, but Grandpa and Dad took it well albeit feeling sad like everyone over the drastic change.

I remember very little about Tien-Yen, but I enjoy listening to stories about our hometown shared by Mom and Dad. My earliest childhood memories were our lives in Ha-Noi, the capital of North Vietnam. Ha-Noi was a modern city of 1.2 million people at the time. Streets were clean and well paved. Crime was minimal and people were friendly and humble.

Grandpa bought a four-story house across from Sword Lake of Ha-Noi, which became the new hub of his scaled-down trucking company. The house had a garden in front and a separate kitchen in the back. The garage was on the far left side of the property. An iron gate was at the center with a pathway winding through the garden to the main entrance of our house. We had a cook, a chauffeur, a gardener and two servants. It was a four-unit 8,000 square foot house with many rooms, so three of my uncles and Aunt Le-Quan also lived with us. The dinner table was large enough to accommodate all; we usually had two servants waiting on us when we had our meals.

Uncle Wing often had parties on the rooftop terrace that had reddish terra-cotta tile floor. Loud music and partygoers' laughter drifted up into the night sky when there was a party going on. Chi and I would pretend to dance like the partygoers after they left; we slid and glided on the left over slippery powder spread by Uncle Wing for people to dance over the tile floor.

Uncle Wing was tall, good-looking and always well dressed. He listened to classical music and liked to paint; the paintings hung in his house in Hong-Kong resembled the works of well-known artists.

My brother David was born in 1953 at a hospital not far from our house in Ha-Noi. He learned to walk on the long balcony overlooking the front garden from one end of the house to the other. Mom planted flowers and vines in containers hanging from the balcony. David was my only brother at the time, so everyone called him "little brother," including Grandpa. This nickname stays with him to this day.

Although Chi is one year older than me, we started kindergarten together at a private school in Ha-Noi. As the privilege of a wealthy family, the school bus driver reserved the two front seats exclusively for Chi and me. Sister Ping was assigned to watch over us, so she came with us to school everyday and waited in the courtyard while Chi and I were in class. Sadly, Ping did not have the opportunity to attend school because of her adopted status.

Aunt Le-Quan is Dad's youngest sister; Mom said she used to take her shopping by taxi or Vietnamese cyclo – a tricycle with comfortable cushioned seat that could seat two adults between two big wheels in front and the driver sitting up high in the back paddling. Mom took good care of her when Aunt Le-Quan was having treatment for her lung problem, so they were very close.

Dad continued to assist Grandpa in running his business, but the business began dwindling with less and less French presence. Our fleet went from 50+ ten-ton trucks to three by the time we moved to Hai-Phong – a major port city along the South China Sea. Grandpa sort of drifted into a retired status. While the downturn was obvious to everyone, it seemed no one wanted to talk about what was going to happen next. The remaining trucks stayed idle with the final drawdown of French troops.

Our house in Hai-Phong was much smaller than the one in Ha-Noi, and it was on a busy street. Because the house number was 123, everyone referred to that house as "123", but I was not old enough to remember the name of the street. It had a huge backyard with big trees; we sat under their shade on hot summer days. Uncle Wing often took me to town on his bicycle and I enjoyed riding in the back cruising down the street. I remember him reminiscing aloud and saying, "I miss those dinner parties we had in Ha-Noi."

Now that he had a lot of time on his hand, Dad took everyone to the beach during the warm summer days in our family Peugeot van that could seat up to 12 people. Chi, Kum, and I loved playing with the sand on the beach.

Uncle Chin, who was a few years younger than Dad, landed a job with an American publishing company that published a Chinese version of one of its magazines, *"Today's World"*; its articles were about current events around the globe. Uncle Chin was bald and chunky; he was not very friendly so we tried to stay away from him as much as possible. Because he always looked angry, his siblings gave him the nickname of "burned-pig-face" that depicted an unhappy fellow. His employer relocated him to Saigon, the capital of South Vietnam, in 1954.

Uncle Wing and Uncle Wah (grandpa's two youngest sons) went back to China for their college education and stayed through the Chinese Cultural Revolution led by Chairman Mao. Uncle Wing wrote grandpa from time to time about the tough time he and his brother went through. They spent the money they brought with them to buy bicycles, their only means of transportation. Everything was rationed under the communist regime.

After graduating with a degree in architecture, Uncle Wing finally made it back to Hong Kong with Uncle Wah, who also got his college degree. Their lives got better with well-paying jobs in Hong-Kong and marriages to their dream girls from college.

The formation of the South-East Asia Treaty Organization (SEATO) in 1954 brought South Vietnam under the American security umbrella like the Philippines, Taiwan, and South Korea[2]. The division of Vietnam into two internationally recognized states that had contrasting political affiliation – the Communist North Vietnam and the Democratic South Vietnam backed by the United States of America.

---

[2]   The Book "History of Vietnamese-Chinese" by Mr. Lieu Nguyen

Grandpa and Dad gave up everything to avoid being labeled as "capitalists" with the history of running a sizable company that had a business relationship with the French government. People in North Vietnam heard about horror stories of businessmen and property owners being sent to re-education camps, a.k.a. labor camps, during the Cultural Revolution. There were also speculations of isolation after "closing of the iron-curtain."

A 300-day window was part of the agreement for people to choose on which side of Vietnam they wished to live. With no prospect of a united Vietnam in the foreseeable future, many ethnic Chinese business owners gave up everything to go south for fear of being targeted by the Communist regime. An exodus of refugees began flowing from North Vietnam to South Vietnam.

The American government aided in evacuating those who chose to leave North Vietnam. Grandpa left early by plane to set up camp in Saigon, and Dad shut down the family business and closed out the bank account. He packed all of our belongings into the three remaining trucks and loaded them onto the military vessel provided by the American Navy, along with a few thousand fellow evacuees, in 1954. The concern and uncertainty was visible in everyone's face.

Mom made rice cakes that could last for days without refrigeration and prepared dried food for the three-day journey down south from the port of Hai-Phong. All the families spread out on the floors of several decks of the ship for this short trip. I was too young to realize the magnitude of the situation and thought we were on a grand vacation. I almost got lost running up and down different decks to explore the biggest ship I had ever seen. I found the row of white ceramic urinals on the wall of a huge men's bathroom fascinating at the time.

Our ship arrived in Saigon on the third day and docked at Ben-Back-Dang – Saigon's deepest seaport along a busy street. The South Vietnamese officials came onboard and quickly completed the immigration process. Self-sufficient families that did not require public housing and government assistance were the first group to disembark; our family was among them because we were going to stay with Grandpa.

From the window of our bus, it was the first time I saw this modern city with many French colonial buildings. Busy streets were filled with people and cars. The elegant tree-lined streets were clean and well kept; even the bottom section of the tree trunks were painted white and looked uniformed.

"Wow, this is what a modern city looks like!" I said to myself.
It was also then I first noticed the beauty of traditional Vietnamese long dresses worn by women on the street. The full-length gown split at the side with the front and back flowing over their white pants – so attractive!

With strong support of the West, especially the U.S., Ngo-Dinh-Diem was made president of the South Vietnamese Government on June 25th, 1954. He forced all Chinese immigrants to become Vietnamese citizens. Those who refused to comply would be required to pay heavy taxes or be deported; every adult in our family got their Vietnamese nationality in 1954. Voting rights also meant military duty for young men.

Chapter 2

New Life in the South

We moved in with Grandpa and lived in Cho-Lon, a suburb of Saigon known as Chinatown, where the vast majority of the population was Chinese. The house Grandpa rented was located behind the gigantic Cho-Lon Market, and it was on the bank of the Cho-Lon River. The location was ideal because there were shops across the street, and a school for my sister and me was just across the narrow river from our house. It was, however, a drastic change from the big houses in which we used to live in North Vietnam. I sensed we were now in the working class group and remembered feeling sorry for Mom and Dad. Grandpa seemed to be taking it well; he spent most of his day playing chess with the landlord downstairs.

My sisters and I took the 5-cent man-powered ferryboat everyday crossing the river to school. The toilet of our house was built on the section stretching over the riverbank; I could see fish swimming underneath when I pooped. When I was not busy with my homework, I snuck out and walked around the market. The market was wet and smelly, especially around the seafood and meat stalls, but I enjoyed watching the live fish display in front of the seafood stores and envisioned them swimming in my imaginary fish-tank at home.

"Mom, can I go across the street for a while?" I asked.

"Don't be long and don't be late for dinner!" she warned.

"Yes, Mom," I said on my way to the front door.

With no playground near our house, I walked to a variety of shops across the street when I was bored. Some of them sold household products, and some of them were small mom-and-pop grocery stores. The candy and cookie stores were the ones that I frequented most of the time. Soft, chewy peanut candies were my favorite; the creamy condensed milk melting in my mouth and the crunchy peanuts were the perfect combination to me. The storeowners became friendlier to me after I had made a few purchases.

Being new to the South, it was difficult for Dad to secure business for our trucks because no one would trust a new guy in town with a truckload of goods. Sometimes Dad let me ride along in his truck; I watched in admiration as he shifted through the gears. I loved hearing the roar of the engine and the smell of gasoline – I knew trucking was in my blood. I still take a second look at beautiful trucks when I see them on the road; only a true trucker can appreciate that.

As his bank account got smaller, Dad began selling the trucks – one at a time. He swapped the last truck for a taxi and became a taxi driver to support our family. The taxi was a 4-door, 28-horsepower Renault 4-CV, with a top speed of only 63 mph. There were a lot of French made vehicles in Vietnam, including Peugeots and Citroens.

I began hearing serious discussions between Mom and Dad about our financial situation. Dad began showing his age and was always in deep thoughts when he came home in the evening during those days. As the head of a Chinese family back then, he bore the sole responsibility of providing for his family and would not allow his wife to work. I knew Dad worried about our future and had never been in the situation of financial struggle because of his success in the past. He was trying his best and never complained about the hardship he had to endure. Living a life of hardship was a scary thought especially we had just started our new lives in the South. What would the future hold?

With no servants to assist her, Mom had to cook and maintain the house. Without a refrigerator she had to shop at the market every morning to prepare meals. She washed our clothes by hand. She also had to take care of Grandpa and all of us; Mom had never had to do any housework before. She seemed to be handling the tasks well; maybe that was the way to show Dad her support.

"Kids, we are going to move. Your Dad and I have worked out your transfers to the new school," Mom said to us one evening over dinner.

"Why?" I asked.
"Because the rent is cheaper, and we will have the entire house to ourselves," Dad responded.
"Is it far from here?" Chi asked.
"It's just in the next precinct," Mom replied.
It was an average residential area without the busy shops and market around us, so it took a little getting used to. There was really nothing for us to do except play in the small front yard by ourselves. Dad had to take Mom to shop for food and household essentials with his taxi twice a week.

THE PHU-BINH COMPLEX

Dad's taxi barely made enough to support our family. With the help of his friend, Dad applied for public housing in the Phu-Binh complex of the 6th Precinct. His application was finally granted after a couple of years on the waiting list.
"It was approved." Dad shared the good news when he got home from his taxi run one day.
"Great. When are we going to move?" Mom exclaimed.
"They said the house should be ready in a couple of weeks."
"How wonderful." Mom had not been that happy for a long time.

Phu-Binh was a government subsidized housing complex built with grants specifically for refugees from the North. The complex had a huge church, a Vietnamese elementary school, a small man-made lake, as well as an open field as playground for the kids. There was an open market at the entrance to serve the residents of the complex.

There were approximately 300 families living in rows and rows of houses built in square blocks of narrow streets. These were little townhouses with common walls and just one bathroom. There were 10 houses in each row with no front or backyard. It was a flat with no rooms, so Dad put up walls to make a bedroom for him and Mom. He added a loft above the bedroom as sleeping quarter for us in addition to two bunk beds in the living room, which was open to the front door. We only had basic furniture – a folding dinning table and folding chairs. An old sofa took up one side of the small living room, and our dining table was on the other side by the front window overlooking the street.

There was no running water, so wells were dug at strategic locations to provide water for the residents. There was no flush toilet, just a kind of chamber pot in the back of the house. The small kitchen had only a wood-burning stove and a screened cupboard to store dinnerware and left over food. It was dark and damp and cluttered. There was no bathtub or shower; we had to heat water and pour it into a bucket to wash ourselves with towel and soap. During summer we just bathed with cold water fetched from the well. We didn't have shampoo; a bar of soap was all we got.

It seemed to me our standard of living had gone from bad to worse as we moved further away from the city. Dad had gone from a successful businessman to a taxi driver with no money in his bank account; Mom had to take care of us in a low-income complex. Luxury was a thing of the past, and I didn't know when things were going to turn around. I was fearful that it was going to get worse!

In order not to be a burden on my parents, I just went with the flow without saying anything. Chi and I helped out with chopping wood and stacking it underneath the stoves for Mom to use for cooking. Wet wood had to be dried in the sun so it would be easier to burn and produce less smoke.

The new house provided by the Vietnamese government was very small for our family, so Grandpa moved in with Uncle Chin who lived in a nice condo in town. Grandpa came to see us every Sunday and stayed until after dinner before taking a cyclo ride back to his house. We gathered around him and held his hands when he arrived. Grandpa always asked about our grades and if we were obedient to Mom and Dad. We waited for the usual two Piasters that he gave us as spending money every Sunday and ran to the convenient store to buy candies or cookies. Grandpa was kind and caring; I always looked forward to his visit – and the two Piasters.

Including Ping, I have a total of eight brothers and four sisters. Mom and Dad kept having kids until they had 9 boys: me, David, Choi, Ken, Keith, Bill, Tom, John and Bob; and 3 girls: Chi, Kum and Nora (we didn't have American names until we moved to the U.S.). With the adopted girl (Ping), our family grew from 7 to a whopping 15 with only Dad's income as a taxi owner/driver to support the entire family. He barely made ends meet, so Dad sold his taxi to a businessman and leased it back from him in order to supplement his small income from the taxi fare.

Fighting and arguing were inevitable with so many siblings living in a small house, but we got over them quickly and actually cared a lot for one another. The older children helped taking care of the younger siblings to lighten Mom's workload, including bathing them. Although Mom and Dad did not ration food, they kept a watchful eye at the dinner table to make sure we all had our equal share. While waiting for the green light from Mom to start, we all had our chopsticks ready for the best piece of chicken or meat we had our eyes on when the dish was first set on the table. We had to be quick but subtle because punishment for bad table manners would mean less good things to eat.

Fortunately we didn't have any major medical problems except for the occasional cold and flu, and those were a quick fix with a trip to the doctor in town. I don't remember seeing a dentist in South Vietnam; extraction of a bad tooth was wiggling to loosen it before pulling it out ourselves with a string.

Without a refrigerator and no supermarkets, Mom went to the local open market every morning to buy what was needed and would be cooked that day. Beef and chicken were luxury items that we could only have once a week. There were no frozen or pre-slaughtered chickens, so Mom bought live chickens and killed them herself.

"Go fetch a bowl and a knife quickly," Mom told me. She held the chicken's wings together on its back and bent its head backward.

"Put the bowl here," Mom pointed to the spot in front of her. The chicken struggled to get free, but Mom held it so tight it couldn't go anywhere. Mom picked up the knife and sliced into the chicken's neck. Blood spewed out from the chicken's open gash and dripped into the bowl. "Okay, help me clean it," Mom ordered.
I helped pluck the feathers after dipping the dead chicken in boiling water to make the process easier. I later learned how to slaughter a chicken by myself and took over the task from Mom.

One chicken, cut into bite-size pieces, fed the entire family with stir-fried vegetables and steamed rice. Every piece of organ and every part of the chicken, including neck, head and feet, were used so nothing went to waste. Drumsticks were considered the best part, and they were reserved only for the youngest kids in the family (John and Bob). I was of the opinion that the treatment was unfair to the older ones.

We didn't have running water either. Mom had to get water from a nearby public well and carry two buckets at a time to the house. To accomplish this, she carried a piece of wood five feet long across her shoulders. On each end of the plank was a hook to hold the bucket handle. We helped out with this labor-intensive task when we got older. Dad built two water tanks to store water: one for drinking and cooking, the other for washing clothes and bathing. Dad later had a private well dug in front of our house for our own use.

We made our own toys with scrap wood or empty metal cans to play with kids in the neighborhood. We made spinning tops by shaping a short section of a tree branch about two inches in diameter with a sharp knife. We then drove a big nail into the narrower end. We cut off the head of the nail and sharpened it with stone. Once done, we used the sharp end to break other kids' tops by slamming ours on their spinning tops in contest and games. Wood from guava trees was the preferred choice because it's hard enough to withstand a lot of abuse. We also engaged in marble competitions, where the winner took the marbles of the losers. In a short time, I had a big box of marbles from the games I won.

We made toy trucks with wood and made the tires with beer or soda bottle caps tied to an axle made out of chopsticks. Using left over steamed-rice as glue, we made lanterns by gluing see-through colored paper to shells made with thin bamboo sticks and lit them with candles at night. Creative shapes from animals to star were seen during the August Moon Festival. We applied the same technique to build kites and compete in flying them as high as we could.

We were poor from financial perspective, but we had a very memorable and happy childhood. While I used to have nice toys in North Vietnam when the family business was thriving, but playing and competing with other kids with the toys I made myself was more satisfying. I learned a lot from them and loved the neighborhood feel of things – I felt free.

When cousin Khang came to visit, we would team up to play against other kids. Khang was my best partner; I always made sure he was on my team whenever we played team sports, such as ping-pong, soccer and basketball. We didn't have well-paved fields so we just found an empty, level spot and drew our makeshift court. We had a lot of fun; the added bonus was Khang and I were often on the winning team.

There was a movie theater within walking distance of our house; I was allowed to see a movie once in a while. Dad liked country western cowboy movies, but they were shown in bigger and more expensive theaters in town. Because money was tight, he took us there only on special occasions.

We also raised chickens and ducks as pets. I remembered Mom bought me two little baby ducks, and I had to feed them daily. When they got bigger, I let the ducks out of the cage in the morning and they ate whatever they could find during the day. Somehow, they could find their way home and would come back before sunset to the cage I placed in front of our house.

"Don, don't let the ducks out today," Dad said to me one morning.
"Why?" I asked.
"You and I are going to take them to Uncle Chin as his birthday gift this afternoon," Dad replied.
I ran outside and cried. I stopped when Mom explained that Dad was trying to save money from buying a present. My ducks became one of the dinner party dishes that week.

Because of the large Chinese population, there were two school systems in Vietnam – Chinese and Vietnamese. Virtually all of the Chinese children went to Chinese schools that taught exclusively in Mandarin. Our family came from Guangdong (Canton, China), so we spoke Cantonese at home, and we learned to speak Mandarin in school.

The Vietnamese at the time did not put as much emphasis in education or business work compared to the Chinese; therefore, the vast majority of the businesses were owned and operated by the Chinese in Vietnam. Although we seemed to coexist in harmony, there was an underlying ethnic tension and animosity between the Vietnamese and Chinese in Vietnam. Vietnamese officials often had to be bribed by the Chinese businessmen to get timely approval of building permits, custom clearances, and business licenses, etc.

Yam-Zin Chinese elementary school was approximately two miles from our house; we all attended that school before going to the larger Shuay-Sang Chinese school in Chinatown. About 10 miles from our house, the school had classes from 1st to 12th grade. Yam-Zin was very small; it had only four classrooms for grade 1 to 4, with a small playground and a public restroom in the back.

A distant relative of ours taught in Shuay-Sang Chinese school. He made the arrangement for Chi and me to start 5th grade there (Chi is a year older than me, but I am not sure why we ended up in the same grade). Dad took us to school the first day in his taxi; I was nervous but excited about going to a big school that had more than two thousand students. A school uniform was required, and we all looked like boy/girl scouts in our khaki uniforms.

"Are you excited about going to a big school, Don?" Dad asked.
"A little nervous," I whispered.
"How about you, Chi?"
"I am fine. I am a big girl now. I will look after Don." Chi looked at me and gave me a vote-of-confidence smile. Though she was only a year older, Chi often acted as if she knew more than I did. Initially I was intimidated by the size of the school and the students around me, but I got used to it after a few weeks.

Grandpa's condo was just a few blocks from the school, so Chi and I had lunch with him on school days. Grandpa often slipped us a buck or two for ice cream or candies on our way back to school for the afternoon classes. Shaved ice drinks were my favorite in the hot summer days, but they were a little more expensive than we could afford.

There was no public transportation that served our area. Chi and I took a horse-drawn cart that cost 2 Piasters per person to school. It had bench seats along each side of the cart that could accommodate up to eight passengers, with the driver sitting up front directing the single horse that pulled the cart. It had two big wooden wheels (like those carriages in Western cowboy movies), and there was a shelf on the outside of the cart on each side for small items brought along by the passengers.

I hated being stuck in the middle seat where passengers sat touching shoulder-to-shoulder and rubbing knees with the person sitting on the opposite side. There were three little square windows at shoulder level and a metal step in the back for the passengers to get onto the cart from the rear opening. When it rained, the driver would unroll a tarp over the windows and the front, but the rear remained wide open.

If there were empty seats (it could seat four on each side), the driver would pick up passengers along the way to fill the spots. It was such a relief when I was old enough to ride my bike to school.

The local church had classes during summer teaching Vietnamese, so Dad sent me there to learn. Soon I learned to say prayers in Vietnamese led by our teachers every morning, and I became proficient in Vietnamese after a few years.

Our Vietnamese teacher organized camping for the students during Christmas holidays every year.

"We will set up tents behind the church the day before Christmas, and we will spend Christmas Eve together as a group," the teacher announced. "I will show you how."
"Yes, Sir." We were all excited and couldn't wait to get started.
We gathered on the lawn behind the church, and our teacher showed us how to remove the grass with a shovel. We followed his instructions to clear a spot for each tent before erecting them. After we had dug up the grass, we placed a straw mat in the center to keep the dirt out.
"Drive these in with a hammer," our teacher gave us the spikes and pointed out the proper locations.
"You two go to each side and hold up the tent," he ordered two of my classmates and pulled the rope towards me.
"Tie it to the spike, Don."
"Yes, Sir."
Viola! My first camping tent was completed.

We hung the lights around our tents and spent Christmas Eve under the moonlight. We built a fire and gathered to sing and dance. Sunlight woke me up, and I didn't even know when I fell asleep. It was my first camping trip and a night I will never forget.

My Vietnamese teacher told us that the Vietnamese alphabet was invented by a French priest named Alexandre Rodes. Chinese language was the foundation of the Vietnamese language, and actual Chinese characters were used in written form until Alexandre Rodes combined the Vietnamese pronunciation with western alphabets to create today's Vietnamese words during the early 18ᵗʰ century. In addition to my Chinese name (Lao Coc Tong), I also used Lao-Hung-Hanh as my Vietnamese name – Asian sur-name goes first and first name last. I am proud of my heritage as a Chinese and viewed myself as a foreigner in Vietnam, but I fully respected the Vietnamese.

I didn't have a sense of where I belonged. I am Chinese born in Vietnam, yet I was not a Chinese citizen; I am Vietnamese, yet I was treated as a foreigner. I felt like I was a person without a nationality.

Dad finally gave up driving the taxi and joined a group of his friends in the textile business. They each owned a few semi-automated weaving machines that chucked out simple pattern fabrics. A wholesaler came to our part of town every week to buy whatever we could produce.

Chi and I helped operate weaving machines during summers and when we were not in school. We actually became very skillful and learned how to weave plaid fabric with different color threads. When manning the machine for single color fabrics, we would let the shuttle go until it ran out of thread before we changed it out. Multi-color fabrics required switching shuttles with different color threads at certain intervals. We learned to slow down the machine and switch the shuttle after 10 to 20 runs, depending on how many lines of threads that color pattern needed for the design.

While holding a shuttle of a different color thread with our left hand, we would slow down the machine and catch the running shuttle with our right hand without stopping the machine completely (like the scene in the movie "*Wanted*" where Angelina Jolie was training her apprentice, James McAvoy, but we caught the shuttle when it exited at the end, not in the middle). We then shoved in the one in our left hand at lightning speed to switch color while pushing the restart button to get the machine back to normal speed without stopping the machine. We would stand there and repeat this function until our shift ended.

My brother Choi was the first boy born in South Vietnam (1955), followed by Ken (1956), and Keith (1958). Choi was quiet and never caused any trouble, but we could never figure out what he was up to; he was like the forgotten one. My sister, Nora, was born on New Year's Day of 1961.

The streak of children finally came to an end after my parents had Bill (1963), Tom (1965), John (1967) and Bob (1970).

On a hot summer day, I saw people running towards the man-made lake near our house and I followed them to see what was happening.
"They are trying to find the boy!" an elderly man said to the gathering crowd.
"Whose kid? Do you know?" someone asked.
"No one knows."
"They got him! There! There!" people yelled.
I elbowed my way to the front and saw a terrible scene! It was Choi breathless on the ground; he was all wet and his hair stuck to his forehead.
"Please save him!" I screamed to the man performing CPR, "Please! Please!"
My entire body went numb and I was shaking helplessly. The man turned around and said, "Sorry, kid. It's too late."
"No! No! Please do something." I continued to scream. "Breathe, Choi, Breathe."
My mind went blank and I couldn't think. I didn't remember what happened next.

My sister Kum died of an illness in 1956 before we moved to the Phu-Binh complex, and brother Choi died when swimming in the man-made lake near our house. I don't remember much about Kum's death, but I vividly remember Dad curled up on the floor weeping when he returned home from his taxi run the day Choi died. Nothing could be more tragic than the sudden loss of a child of your own.

The whole family was overwhelmed by sorrow and I couldn't believe we lost a loving brother just like that. A simple burial was held in the cemetery nearby later that week.

Grandpa was healthy his entire life until he passed away at the age of 75 in 1962. He died peacefully in his sleep while he was in the hospital due to pneumonia. His funeral was an elaborated one with a dragon hearse – one that well-off Chinese people used in Vietnam for their deceased family member. There were a lot of people who attended the funeral. They walked behind the dragon hearse from his house to the cemetery.

Grandpa was an important person in our lives – he was our inspiration. His passing was an impactful moment for all of us, especially Dad who had been by his side from China to Vietnam and assisted him with his business. To me, he was a kind and caring grandfather who had my utmost respect and admiration. It was hard to believe he had left us, but his legacy will live on in our hearts.

On November 1st, 1963, the Ngo-Dinh-Diem regime was toppled by a group of military leaders headed by General Duong-Van-Minh. President Ngo and his brother were taken from the presidential palace in an M-133 tank, and they were killed inside the tank by the lieutenant assigned to escort them. I didn't know or care much about politics, but the Ngo administration implemented many good programs to enhance the lives of its citizens, including the most popular "Field-for-Farmer" program that benefited many hardworking farmers. He also introduced the low-rent taxi program to help struggling taxi drivers like Dad.

With increasing American involvement and troop build-up, Dad wanted me to learn English so I might have a better chance to land a good job with American government agencies or American companies. Dad made sure that we had the best education possible, so he sent me to a prestigious private English school – the Khai-Tri English High School of Cho-Lon.

In addition to teachers from English-speaking countries, local teachers were college graduates from abroad. The school's uniform was white pants and a white shirt for boys and a white dress for girls. Mom bought me two sets of this uniform, and I washed and ironed them myself. I was very careful with them and tried my best to keep them clean. All the students carried handkerchiefs to cover their seats before sitting down in order to avoid staining the white uniform.

Dad was so impressed with my English when I told him I heard on the American Arm Forces radio that President John F. Kennedy was assassinated on November 22nd, 1963. He asked if I was sure about the shocking news and was a little doubtful about my English initially until the news was in the Chinese newspapers the following day.

I knew Dad was pleased to see my progress and reiterated the importance of education to me.

"Don, education is the most important thing in one's life. I will do whatever it takes to make sure you have a good education."
"Thanks, Dad. I won't let you down."
"Good! Remember: Education, education, education," Dad reiterated. "Knowledge is wealth and power. Things you learn in school are important, but you can also learn from your job and the people around you."

With Dad's encouragement, I was determined to learn as much as I could. I would spend hours in the library reading English newspapers and magazines to improve my English. I also learned from watching American TV and listening to American songs. I found American English is far more soothing than the British accent, and I tried to speak the American way. Learning English became my obsession.

Dad's friend got him a job with the Japanese company that was building the very first hydroelectric power plant for Vietnam. The Nippon Koei Construction firm was contracted by the Japanese government to complete this project as a WWII compensation to Vietnam. They relocated Dad to Da-Rang, a small town in central Vietnam's mountainous region where the power plant was being built. A dam was constructed to build up the water level from the main river running through town. The second major step was digging a tunnel through the mountain to redirect water to two giant pipes down the mountainside to the hydropower plant constructed in the valley below. It took five years to complete the project with 300 kilometers of high wattage power lines to deliver power to Saigon and nearby cities.

The Japanese company provided housing for Dad and the workers Dad hired for them. Mom and everyone in the family except Ping, Chi, David and me moved to live with Dad while he was there. Three of us stayed in Saigon to go to school, and sister Ping was assigned to take care of us. We looked forward to every summer when we were able to join everyone in Da-Rang. There, the weather was milder with mountains and trees, the scenery was beautiful. Dad taught us how to swim and fish and let us go to the only movie theater in town once a week. Dad was an excellent swimmer; we all admired his ability in swimming against the current. His free-style strokes looked like a professional swimmer. He said he wanted to us to become good swimmers so Choi's drowning tragedy would not happen again.

While Dad was at work, we would go up the mountain behind the house and pick wild fruits to eat. There were grapefruit and mango trees but fruits from trees we didn't recognize had a nasty taste, probably because they were not ripe when we picked them. My favorite were the mango trees, which produced ample sweet mangos for us to sample. I still have fond memories of Da-Rang and the relaxed country lifestyle.

The engineers from Japan lived in a more upscale housing complex nearby and they had a bathhouse where they boiled water in a large wooden hot tub that could hold up to three adults. After the Japanese had their baths in the evening, David and I would sneak up to the bathhouse and jump into the hot tub to have fun while the water was still warm. Dad finally caught up with us and put an end to the unhealthy and childish act.

After the completion of the hydropower plant project, the Japanese company moved their operation back to Saigon, providing only technical oversight. When the power plant was handed over to the Vietnamese government in 1966, Dad was transferred back to the Saigon office later that year.

After dating a fine gentleman in the same neighborhood, Ping got married and moved in with her husband. He was small (5'5" and 130 pounds) and did not have a lot of hair, but he had a contagious friendly smile. We all liked him and were happy for Ping. Their first child was a girl, and they ended up having six girls and a son.

After she graduated from high school, Chi had to get a job to help support the family. She worked as a waitress at Hong Kong Restaurant, where they served only American soldiers. Chi was so pretty, and everyone liked her, especially a young American lieutenant from California named Roger Story. Roger became good friends with Chi and our family.

ROADSIDE BOMBS

Each and every building occupied by the foreigners, especially the Americans, was barricaded because of bombings carried out by the Viet-Cong (Communist Vietnamese soldiers who also called themselves The Liberation Force) throughout major cities in South Vietnam. Bars and restaurants frequented by the American soldiers were their favorite targets. The two-way street along the old American Embassy was turned into one-way with the other half of the road blocked off with huge concrete barriers.

"Cong" in Vietnamese means communist. All the foreigners referred to them as VC, Vietnamese Communists.

The VC would place bombs near the perimeter or the entrance of a building and set them off at peak traffic hours. Bombs were also thrown from fast-moving motorcycles going by the buildings. News of Americans and innocent passers-by killed by roadside bombs was reported almost every week. Dad specifically instructed us to avoid going near those places; we often worried about Chi working at the Hong Kong Restaurant serving American soldiers, as it could be the VC's prime target. Many innocent people in the South lost their lives as a result of those incidents. Although reports of violent incidents became routine, it certainly did not alter the pain and tragedy endured by countless families.

Roger shared with us his experience of a car bomb going off at his building. This is Roger's account of the bombing incident he experienced:

> *"March 31st, 1966 was payday, and it was also a Vietnamese holiday. After getting paid, I went to the supply center and assumed the duty, standing by just in case some urgent business came up. At the end of the day I rode the bus to Hong-Kong restaurant, as I always do, and ate dinner. Then I caught another bus to my hotel apartment – The Victoria Building, where I settled down in a chair to do some reading. That day I received my weekly copy of a Seattle newspaper, so I spent the entire evening reading it and contemplating my next duty station and my future plans. At one point, I distinctly remember my mind wandered to the ever-present thought of the possibility of the hotel being bombed. I looked at the drawn blinds and closed curtains, which everybody thought would keep the window glass from flying across the room, and I thought my apartment seemed like such a peaceful and comfortable place. There can be no fear in the city because the danger is always there and you can't be afraid all the time. So you just figure that if something is going to happen it will happen, and if you are lucky, it won't happen to you.*
>
> *I finished the newspaper and thought about picking up "The Oxford History of the American People", but my eyelids were heavy, so I decided to go to bed. I never use an alarm clock because I have a way of waking up when I am supposed to,*

but occasionally I will wake up an hour or two earlier. Friday morning I woke up and glanced at my watch at 4:10 a.m. I was quite pleased because I could go back to sleep until 6:15. The next thing I was aware of was loud automatic weapons fire in the street outside my window. As I had rehearsed in my mind many times I rolled out of bed away from the window and onto the floor. Then I reached up and pulled my pillow down over my head. The firing continued along with several small explosions that sounded as if they were down the street, and then there was a loud explosion that broke a small window glass. I said to myself, "that wasn't so bad". I raised up on my hands and knees trying to get up, but I decided to stay down a little longer. While I was in the act of adjusting my pillow, there was a very bright flash and the door flew open. My side and back felt like I had been shot, and that was all I was aware of in that instant. I tested my muscles and limbs to see if they were all still there. I looked down on my side and saw my cuts and scratches with a little blood streaming out but it didn't look serious. I was sort of amazed that I was still alive so I forgot about my injury and stood up. It was only then I noticed that my room was a total wreck; the walls and ceiling were cracked, windows and frames were gone. The blinds and curtains had vanished, and the wall area below the windows was demolished. The floor was covered with bricks, plaster, chunks of concrete, splintered glass and books and papers were all torn or shredded. The doors to the bathroom and hallway were blown off hinges and splintered. There was a six-foot diameter hole through the bathroom with the remaining wall pushed out into the hallway by at least a foot. So it appeared the main force of the explosion went over me, and most of the debris was absorbed by the bed. I groped around and found a pair of pants in the rubble and pulled them on. I found my boots and poured the glass out of them and put them on.

I could hear wailing and moaning and saw the gas station across the street was on fire and there were piles of rubble where a row of houses next to the gas station had stood.

A major from next door looked in and asked if I was all right. I said, "Yes", but I couldn't find my glasses so I couldn't see well enough to go anywhere. I uncovered the smashed little nightstand on the window side of my bed and found my spare pair of glasses. I climbed over the rubble and went up and down the hallway looking into each room to see if everybody was able to get out on their own. The major saw my bleeding but I couldn't figure out where it was coming from. By then some MPs (military police) had made it up to the second floor and told us to evacuate. I went back to my room to find a shirt and just my luck I also found my wallet laying on the floor under my bed. We all went down the stairwell single file, leaving room for stretcher-bearers to carry out the wounded who couldn't walk. The elevator was blown clear out of the building and there was water cascading down the shaft from broken water pipes.

The stairwell was all that was intact as the blast had blown down all the walls and you could see through the building. Once out in the street, I didn't know where to go. I didn't think I was hurt bad enough to go to the hospital – I would just take up space that should be used by the badly injured. So I thought I would go to the Hong Kong restaurant because Miss Chi would be there and could take care of me. However, the Vietnamese police wouldn't let me go down that way. A U.S. military policeman saw that I was bleeding, so he hailed a jeep to take me to the hospital at top speed, siren blaring. A lot of wounded people were already at the hospital. I went to the ward for walking wounded, and the nurse found a large cut on my posterior that was caused by broken glass or metal. The doctor put in a few stitches and gave me a tetanus shot with some antiseptic on the smaller cuts on my side and back before releasing me. I called my boss and he sent a jeep to pick me up. While I was waiting, an ambulance took away the body of the Vietnamese girl who served us breakfast every morning. I was quite sad.

My clothes were all bloody and I didn't have anything to wear or clean up with, so the officer that picked me up took me by the clothing store and the PX to buy a few things. I must have been a sight roaming through the store in the shape I was in.

I was taken to a villa in Cho-Lon where I took a shower and went to bed because the wounds started to bleed a little.

A Vietnamese officer and a good friend of mine came to see me the next day; they brought me some really pretty flowers too. I got a tearful phone call from Miss Chi in the afternoon when she found out where I was. She showed up later with a big bouquet of flowers. She sat on the bed and talked to me for a couple of hours and that really cheered me up – she's really a wonderful person.

While I was resting I wrote my parents a letter to let them know what happened and that I was all right. They found all of my belongings except my transistor radio and my .45 caliber pistol.

A few weeks later, the Admiral awarded me the Purple Heart medal for wounds received as a result of enemy action. That was one award I had hoped I wouldn't win – qualifying was kind of painful. The only thing that still bugs me is how everyone says, "Hi Rog, how's your ass?"

"Oh well . . ."

Many American soldiers and innocent civilians lost their lives as a result of these roadside bombs. Roger's story gave us a true picture of the horrible acts carried out by the VC and the dangerous environment both Americans and civilians were exposed to.

Chapter 3
My First Job

Through the assistance of her American friends, Chi landed a job with the American Armed Forces Pacific Exchange (PX) as a stock control clerk in the accounting department. The department manager, Mr. Holt, was pleased with Chi's performance and often rewarded her with products he bought from the PX. American made products were considered luxury items in those days.

After my graduation from high school in 1968, Chi asked Mr. Holt to give me a part-time job at the PX. I worked the night shift in the accounting department while taking college level courses during the day. My office was a single level building between two huge warehouses – each was the size of a football field. An elevated platform designed to unload the Sea-Land trailers shipped from the United States was next to the main gate. This location known as the Saigon Depot was a 24-hour operation with an army of forklifts, which were always busy loading and unloading merchandise.

My duties included checking invoices for accuracy and keeping track of them in a logbook. Five other local nationals and I worked under the supervision of an American officer named John. After a few months,

I was transferred to dayshift and was promoted to a local-national supervisor position because of my proficiency in English. I had a group of Vietnamese national employees reporting to me. My boss was Mr. Cummings, a civilian employee from the U.S.

Chi and I rode the same Honda motorcycle to work. Sometimes Dad would treat us to breakfast at a roadside stand selling "Pho" – the popular Vietnamese beef noodle soup.

"Three bowls of special noodle with raw beef, please," Dad said to the owner/operator and his daughter who was helping him.
"Coming right up," the girl quickly responded.
We sat at a table with a few folding chairs next to the cart where the mobile kitchen was housed.
"Enjoy!" the girl said as she put the bowl of Pho on our table.
She also brought out a plate filled with fresh bean sprouts, lime slices, basil leaves, and sliced fresh chili peppers. Dad and Chi put a little bit of everything in their bowl and stirred up the noodle to cook the raw beef placed on top of it; I don't like hot dishes so I usually left out the chili peppers. We all enjoyed the father and daughter/son gathering that occurred at least once a month.

I was later assigned to the Insurance and Claims Department where we handled claims against Sea-Land Company for damaged and missing merchandise shipped from the state. Sea-Land was the exclusive shipping company for the PX at the time. I loved conducting field investigations with my boss because I was able to go out in a PX vehicle, and eat American food at the commissary that served the American troops. It was the first time I tasted the yummy southern fried chicken and flavorful ice cream.

As part of our claim investigation, we were provided with Polaroid instant photo cameras to take pictures of the damaged merchandise as supporting documents for our claims against the shipper. We sent in claims to the Sea-Land Company along with photos of the shipping containers' broken seals as well as the shipping manifest. Beer and soda were particularly problematic because of the vast quantity and the fact that they could be easily stolen.

I listened to the American Forces Vietnam Network radio and learned to sing American songs. I followed top hits on the Bill-Board Parade and bought vinyl records from the PX with the help of my American colleagues. My boss rewarded me with three new albums when he came back from a vacation in the U.S.: Three Dog Night's "*Joy To The World*", The Partridge Family's "*I Think I Love You*", and Tom Jones's "*Delilah*".

We didn't have a TV so I learned the lyrics by writing down the words as I listened to the songs on the radio and compiled some 400 hit songs. Credence Clearwater Revival (CCR), the Beatles and Glen Campbell were my favorite artists. CCR produced hit after hit in the late 1960's, but I couldn't understand why none of their songs made it to number one. There were so many great songs and great artists, my list grew longer and longer. Those songs played a big part in improving my English; I learned so much from the lyrics and from singing them.

Me and my boss, Mr. Cummings.
Taken at the PX office in Saigon.

My office at the PX in Saigon.

Fast forward to 2006. My son, Steven, who moved to New York City, bought me an Ipod and introduced me to this great invention that can not only store thousands of songs in such a tiny little device, but also lets you select a specific song to play very easily. I especially like the "shuffle" feature, which has the element of pleasant surprise by playing songs randomly, which brings back fond memories. Those songs remind me of the places in Vietnam where I first heard them, especially the great time I had at the PX.

When we stayed in the guesthouse of my Dad's boss, I would sneak up to the main house to catch the "Glen Campbell Hour" on his TV while he was out with my Dad. I had so much fun watching Glen Campbell; I fell in love with all of his songs. He also had guest singers on his show that played my favorite songs.

In addition to American employees, the PX also hired contracted workers from the Philippines and South Korea. I learned a lot from these foreign workers and some of them became my good friends (Michelle, Domagus, Cleo, Nora, Arci, Connie Lee). The office held Christmas parties every year with presents for every local employee; I enjoyed tremendously the privilege of helping my boss in dividing up gifts and packing them for the local employees. The gifts were just nicely wrapped bags full of candies and cookies, but everyone was so excited to receive them.

My American colleague John, a Filipino named Domagus, and I wanted to form a band, so we took lessons at a local music school. John learned to play bass guitar, Domagus learned to play drums. I took electric guitar lessons and bought a used guitar with an amplifier. I still remember Mom complaining of the "noise" I made from playing my electric guitar! The very first song we played was *"California Dreaming"* by *The Mamas & The Papas*. We practiced and played at John's house, but we didn't pursue it because of our busy workload and my school schedule.

John knew I was fascinated with the American lifestyle, so he often talked to me about life in the U.S.

"The United States is truly a free county. We can speak our mind under a democratic society where the sky is the limit for anyone with potential," John said proudly. "It's also a beautiful country with vast resources."
"I live in California where we have sunny weather for beach goers or just a few hours away mountains for hikers and skiers."
"Almost everyone owns a car and many of us have nice houses," John continued. I listened with great interest and enjoyed his company.
"Wouldn't it be nice if I had a chance to go there?" I shared my thoughts with him.
"I am sure you will have the chance some day." He smiled.

The Vietnamese American Association (VAA) was formed by the U.S. government to provide advanced English courses for local students. In addition to advanced English courses, I also took modern American literature at the VAA and was introduced to fine writings of Robert Frost and Ernest Hemingway. I began paying attention to better choice of words by talented writers in books, newspapers and magazines from the VAA student library. One of my mentors at the PX was a Filipino named Arci Sibal, who taught me English business letter writing. He was an English major and an excellent teacher; I learned a lot from him.

Through the help of my American boss, I signed up for college level correspondence courses on accounting and bookkeeping offered by the University of Michigan. I was drawn to the English language and absorbed everything I learned like a sponge. Life at the PX and my continued studies became an obsession and kept me perpetually occupied. It was exciting and satisfying.

THE TET OFFENSIVE

Tet is the Vietnamese New-Year holiday when all the businesses were closed for a few days to celebrate. During the Tet holidays, people pay respect to the elderly by giving them red envelopes with money inside and wishing them well. Every family stocks up on food and drinks for the entire week as most of the stores are closed. Making rice cakes is one of the Chinese traditions followed by the Vietnamese. Rice can be preserved inside their bamboo-leaf wrappings for days. Dried meats are also must-have items during the New-Year holidays. Kids get new clothes and new shoes on New Year's Eve and dress up during the week of Tet; they also receive red envelopes with money inside from their parents and relatives. The front part of every house gets a new coat of paint, and flowers decorate the inside of every home. I remember painting the front door and window with Dad and accompanying him to shop for tangerine plants – tangerines are pronounced as "luck" in Chinese, so every family has at least one tangerine plant in their house during the New Year holidays.

Parents take their kids to visit friends and relatives where they will be greeted with tea, candies and cookies. Tet was our happiest time because we had a lot of good things to eat and collected a lot of money.

The VC took the opportunity in 1968 to launch a full-scale attack when everyone was busy celebrating Tet; it seemed they were in every major city in the south, including Cho-Lon, where we lived (in the 6th precinct). It was strangely quiet on that New Year's Day when we woke up. Tet is also the Chinese New Year as the Vietnamese follow the Chinese calendar and celebrate the same holidays.

"What's going on?" I asked Dad while rubbing my eyes. "Why did you wake us up this early on New Year's Day?"
"Quiet!" Dad led us downstairs.
When dad opened the front door, we could see gunmen in traditional North Vietnamese pajama-like clothing on our street. Everyone panicked because that was the first time we came face-to-face with the VC! My heart was pounding.
"Good morning, Sir." When they saw Dad, they greeted him in a friendly manner and stayed on the street without harassing us.
We saw soldiers as young as 13 with AK-47's slung across their backs. They were so young and short, their rifles almost touched the ground!

"We have to go," Dad turned to Mom and said. "Pack a few things. Quick!"
"Why do we have to go, Dad?" I asked.

"Quiet," Dad said forcefully. "It's not safe for us to stay here. We have to go. Take the motorcycles and let's get out of here now!"

Dad realized it was no longer safe to stay and that we needed to head for the center of town before fighting broke out between the VC and the South Vietnamese soldiers and the American forces. Otherwise we would be caught in the crossfire. We were all frightened; we weren't sure when we would be able to get back to our house or what would happen next, but it was too dangerous to stay behind.

Fortunately the VC's did not block us. Soon after we left, the American helicopter gun-ships circled the area with loud speakers urging civilians to evacuate. We could see rockets raining down from the helicopters behind us, so we sped up and took shelter in a distant relative's (Aunt Fong) house in the 5th precinct.

"Alan, we have cleared out the two bedrooms upstairs for your family," Aunt Fong said.
"Thank you, Fong, for taking us in. It's not easy to find a place for my big family."
"Don't worry about it. This is an unusual time; we are happy to help," Aunt Fong said. "I believe we have enough pillows and blankets for the kids, but let me know if you need anything."

Mom and Dad stayed in one of the bedrooms with John and Bob; Ping, Chi and Nora had the other one. The rest of us slept on the floor. Mom and my sisters helped with the cooking during the day, and Dad instructed us to stay inside the house. Dad and Aunt Fong's husband watched the news on their black-and-white TV. Not only was reception poor, TV programs were broadcasted only for a few hours each day, so they followed the news with a transistor radio. We could hear gunfire and explosions in the distance. My siblings and I were frightened; I worried about what was going to happen to us. I kept the fears to myself because I didn't want to further burden Mom and Dad.

We later learned that this "panorama attack" known as the "Tet Offensive" was launched in the predawn hours of Tet (January 30th,

1968). The military campaign was orchestrated by North Vietnam; the offensive was countrywide and well coordinated with mobilization of more than 80,000 VC and North Vietnamese troops striking more than 100 towns and cities throughout South Vietnam, including the southern capital of Saigon.

The offensive was the largest military operation conducted by either side up to that point in the war. The initial attacks stunned the American and South Vietnamese leaders, and it caught their military units by surprise.

The two major airbases near Saigon – Bien Hoa and Tan-Son-Nhat – were under heavy shelling by the VC with rockets and mortars to prevent American air support. They also occupied the Chinese business district of Cho-Lon and broke down walls between stores to form their defensive position in confrontation with the South Vietnamese army. The whole city was deserted with buildings riddled with bullet holes and blown down walls. They were attempting to seize the presidential palace on Thong-Nhat street in the 1st precinct of Saigon and the nearby radio station; the goal was to collapse the Saigon regime with these military blows and force the U.S. to open negotiations under disadvantageous conditions. A portion of the fighting was shown on the nightly news and heard on the radio.

The fighting intensified and lasted a couple of weeks before the VC, backed by the North Vietnamese troops, were driven out of the cities by the persistent efforts of the South Vietnamese Army and the American Armed Forces.

We returned to our house after the fighting was over a couple of weeks later and found our house survived with only a few bullet holes while many houses in our neighborhood were badly damaged or destroyed. I couldn't imagine being trapped in our house during the intensive fighting between the VC and the South Vietnamese army. Thanks to Dad's quick reaction, we were able to get out in time and were lucky to be alive!

Fighting between the two sides had been going on for years, but the effect of war had never been so close to home. The Chinatown business district looked like Beirut, and the aftermath revealed the widespread damage from Chinatown to Saigon; it took months to rebuild before lives got back to normal.

As the war continued to drag on, I received an order that forced me into military service in 1972, even though I was in an exempt status as a Chinese minority. Dad was scrambling to get me off the hook by contacting influential figures in the military police department through his friends. Mom and Dad were worried sick about the possibility of my being sent to war.

I myself was trying to process what was going to happen to me. I am a Chinese and I don't want to join the Vietnamese forces to fight and kill their own people. I had never held a gun in my life; all I had ever done was kill chickens for family meals. I just wanted to get back to my normal life!

In compliance with the order, I had to report to the nearest police station.

"David, can you take me to the police station?" I asked.

"Of course," David replied. "Let me get my motorcycle ready."

"Wait for me here," I told David when we arrived at the police station near our house.

I walked in and presented the Vietnamese officer with the order I received.

"Let me see your ID and your draft status document," he ordered.

I showed him my exempt certificate and my ID. He examined the documents and said, "I think we need to keep you here until your status is confirmed."

"Why? These are valid documents, officer."

"We need to verify them."

"Wait. If you need time to confirm the documents, can you run a copy and set a time for me to come back?"

"No!" he responded in an angry voice.

I sensed something was terribly wrong. Corrupt Vietnamese police were known to blackmail Chinese of military age; I knew I was in serious trouble.

"My brother is waiting for me outside. I need to let him know," I said to the officer.

"I will go with you." He followed me out to the front entrance.

I walked up to David and said in a barely audible voice, "David, they are keeping me here for investigation. Go get Dad and ask him to do something now!"

"Are you sure?" David couldn't believe what he heard.

"Hurry! We don't have much time."

They put me in a cell after David left and asked me to wait there.

Dad showed up a few hours later and had a long talk with the officer in charge.

"They want $50,000 Dong (Vietnamese Piaster)," Dad walked over to me and said. "We don't have that kind of cash but I have countered with $20,000."

"What did he say?"

"Don't worry. I will work with them to get you out of here," Dad noticed I was a little uneasy and scared.

"Thanks, Dad." I was still concerned about my situation and whether they would let me go.

Dad moved up to $30,000 in cash but they were firm on their demand. Dad told me he would get help from a high-ranking officer to intervene. Unfortunately it took time to get through to a busy officer and we missed the deadline. By the end of the week, I was sent to the training camp in the city of Quan-Trung 30 miles north of Saigon. While Dad continued to work on his end, I was officially drafted and assigned to a new group of young recruits.

Living under the constant threat of being drafted, I dreaded going to training camp and being sent to war since I had reached the military age requirement of 18. Now I had to face the fears and go through what could be the worst experience of my life.

I shared a metal-frame bunk bed with a Vietnamese fellow; I had the upper bed. Along with the uniform, we also received a pillow and a blanket. Instead of a mattress, we got a straw mat.

I couldn't sleep the first night because my entire body was itching badly from insect bites. I traced the problem to the old straw mat, which was infested with bedbugs – I could see them crawling between the poorly woven mat and worn-out straws. I threw it out and slept on the bare metal top instead. It still makes me shudder thinking about it.

Dad tracked down where they sent me and took Mom to see me; weekends were new recruits' visiting days for parents, friends and relatives. An open field at the entrance to the camp was the gathering place for the visitors to catch up with their sons or brothers. Mom cooked things I liked and brought them with her.

"My friend is working on it, but it will take time," Dad filled me in on the progress and tried to comfort me.
"You need to take care of yourself and be careful," Mom kept reminding me.
"I will, Mom."
That was the first time I was away from home and I started to feel homesick.

Because I was tall and strong, the training officer assigned the only M-60 machine gun of our group to me. We marched three miles everyday to the training field. We practiced shooting with our own M-16 rifles on a daily basis; I learned to take apart an M-16 and put it back together in just a couple of minutes. We also learned how to throw grenades and use M-79 grenade launchers; the burned gunpowder odor from exploding grenades and gunfire was suffocating. The M-16 and M-79 were not heavy, but carrying the M-60 machinegun was like having a load of bricks on my shoulder!

We ate lunch wherever we camped out for the day and returned to base camp for dinner. A large bucket of mixed meat and vegetables was placed in the middle of the dining room as the main entrée of our dinner. Once the officer in charge gave the green light, we swarmed the food bucket and tried to scoop up as much as our bowl could hold before going for the steamed rice, which was left for all we could eat on the other side of the dining hall. Our appetite was exceptionally good after walking hours to and from the training field. The stir-fried veggies and meat were not of restaurant quality, but they surely tasted like gourmet dishes to me under the circumstances.

After exhausting every possible way to get me home, Dad resorted to securing a safe assignment for me in Saigon. A friend of Dad's who had connection with the 5th Airborne Division asked the commanding general to transfer me there. The idea was to use his influence for a favorable assignment in town to avoid being sent to the front line.

"Don't worry, son. The war is winding down; you should be okay," Dad said it was no longer a threat because the North and the South Vietnamese governments were negotiating a peace treaty orchestrated by the U.S., Russia and China.

A group of recruiting officers from the 5th Airborne Division came to our camp with a medical team the following week. I was on the list of the 10 recruits they were going to enlist.

"Please line up here," the officer explained. "You have to pass our medical tests before you can join our Airborne Division."
One of the medical team members in a white gown walked up to me and performed his evaluation in front of everybody.
After completing the first phase of his examination, he said, "Drop your pants."
I followed his order and he continued with the physical exam.
"He is good to go," he said to the officer in charge and gave me a copy of the form he signed.
"Pack your things and get on the truck," the officer said to me.
They took me and the selected recruits to the Army base reserved exclusively for the 5th Airborne Division.

I went through basic airborne training, and acquired skills that included how to fold and pack a parachute, proper landing technique for jumping off a 10-foot platform, and propelling down a low-hovering helicopter. The final training consisted of a group parachute jumping off a C-130 military plane. I became buddies with a fellow soldier name Trung, a South Vietnamese. He was short and tiny with thick black hair and big brown eyes. Trung was very optimistic and he always had a smile on his face. We stuck together during and after the daily training.

Everything would have been acceptable except for one miscalculation – the escalation of war! The peace process was not as rosy as it sounded because my Division received orders to ship out to the De-Militarized Zone north of the city of Hue (Central Vietnam) to rotate with the 3rd Airborne Division, which had suffered heavy casualties.

With less than a month of training, we were on our way to the combat zone! We boarded a C-130 and flew from Saigon to a military airbase in Da-Nang, Central Vietnam. After a briefing the following morning, our convoy left Da-Nang and headed north. On our way to the battlefield, I saw wreckage of abandoned armored vehicles and overturned military trucks scattered on both sides of that stretch of Highway One. We continued inland towards the mountainous region of Hue, the most northern city of South Vietnam that bordered North Vietnam.

When we arrived at the war zone, tanks from the 3rd Airborne Division were leaving the area with dead bodies stacked on top of them. I had a bad feeling and said to Trung, "What have we got ourselves into this time?"
"I am scared," He responded in a trembling voice.
"I am too. But there's nothing we can do now," I tried to calm him down. As we walked passed the tanks, I turned away to void looking at the dead soldiers.

When we arrived at the base camp left behind by the 3rd Airborne Division, we dug foxholes and piled sandbags around the foxholes and our tents. Sweat dripped off my forehead under the hot sun, and my hands had blisters from digging and shoveling. I didn't mind the hard labor because the foxhole and the sandbags were for my own safety and protection.

Being in the middle of nowhere, we were given ready-to-eat meals and canned food. We made steamed rice by pouring water into a package of hydrated rice; it tasted so bad, I tossed them out. Trung felt sorry for me and pointed out that we had no choice.

"We need the strength to survive," he said.
Trung mixed the rice with Spam to make it easy for me to eat. I added black pepper to make the nasty taste easier to swallow.

Our camp was on a hilltop along Song-Thach-Han – a river along the 17th parallel, the infamous DMZ (De-Militarized Zone) that divided North and South Vietnam. Trung and I shared a foxhole and we could see and hear the North Vietnamese soldiers and VC on the other side of the river. We set up guard towers around the perimeter and continued to build up the facility that we might need for a while. Our daily activities were often interrupted by mortar shelling from the VC. When we heard "Incoming!" and the whistling sound of bombshells traveling through air, we dove into the foxholes. Shells sometimes got close enough to splatter dirt on top of us.

Trung and I talked about our families and things we would like to do after the war. His parents were small vendors selling produce at local market. He said he had a lovely sister who was in elementary school. Trung wanted to finish high school and attend college when he returned to Saigon; he aspired to be a doctor.

When I was asleep one night, Trung jerked my shoulder and said, "Wake up, it's your turn to stand guard."

I sat up and rubbed the sleep out of my eyes before picking up my helmet and rifle. Hugging the M-16 to my chest, I sat at the guard post in total darkness. Noise of leaves blowing in the wind kept me awake until the next morning.

The same routine went on for about a month before we received an order to launch a surprise attack. Our lieutenant did the prep talk that evening and got us ready for the combat mission.

"Don, I am scared," Trung whispered to me.
"I am too, but everything will be okay," I tried to make him feel better.
"Remember to stay close and don't try to be a hero."
He nodded.

The sky was pitch black and the air was still. All was quiet except the rhythmical chirping of crickets around us while we lined up single file in complete silence with radios off. We marched towards the river and waded across a waist-deep section silently. When we approached the valley, it was exceptionally quiet, until all hell broke loose.

A hail of gunfire from the mountain ridge around us formed strings of lights flying towards us.

"Trung, follow me!" I hollered to Trung.
We ran for cover with our heads down. We got down on the ground and returned fire, shooting blindly in total darkness attempting to aim at the origin of the enemy gunfire. Gunfire crisscrossed across the sky like lightning, and earsplitting explosions of mortar shells were like loud thunders pounding over me. The smell of gunfire reminded me of the practice shooting and grenade launching in the training camp; it was nauseating.

After unloading every bullet that I had on me, I headed for the mountainside and I could hear bullets hitting the ground next to me. I lost track of Trung when I got behind a big piece of big rock and waited for the gunfire to die down. While my heart was pounding, I couldn't stop thinking about the fact that my life was going end soon. The fear of dying was so overwhelming; I started praying and couldn't help thinking that I would never see my family again! I took one of the two grenades hanging on my belt and held it in my right hand as my final line of defense. "Please don't let me be the POW of the VC." I prayed.

That was probably the longest night of my life. The night combat scene of the movie "***Platoon***" by Oliver Stone reminded me of that hellish night.

At first light, I could see bodies all over the place but miraculously I was not hurt. The valley was littered with tree limbs; it looked like the aftermath of a tornado!

"No! No!" I broke down and cried when I saw Trung's corpse with half of his lung blown away. My mind went blank witnessing such a horrifying scene; I didn't know what I was supposed to do or where to go.

"Hey, you. Are you okay?" a fellow paratrooper shouted from a distance.
"Is that you, Don?" he asked when he got closer to me.
I didn't answer.
"It's you. Are you hurt?" he kept asking me.
"I don't know." I shook off his hand when he tried to touch me.
"You lucky son-of-a-bitch. You don't have a scratch on you. Amazing!" he said after running his hand up and down my arms and upper body.
"Are you sure you are okay?" He looked at me and wiped off dirt and fallen leaves from my face and shoulder.
I nodded.
"Are you able to help?" he asked.
I nodded again.
"It's safe now. We called in artillery support last night and drove the VC away," he was trying to comfort me.
We trimmed down tree branches and tied our military-issued raincoats as makeshift stretchers to carry the wounded and dead bodies back to our base camp.

I packed Trung's belongings and gave them to our lieutenant to send along with his body to his family in Saigon; it was a dark day of my life. Trung was so young and full of potential; he had so much to look forward to. It was tragic to see so many young people paid the ultimate price because of the meaningless conflict in Vietnam.

A few weeks later, it was our turn to rotate out, with 60 dead and more that 30 wounded. When I saw the newly arrived 2nd Airborne Division to take over the fighting, I could almost see their fate and I prayed for their safe return. It was tragic to see people of the same country killing each other for nothing. It was hard for me to understand why they couldn't put down their guns and live in harmony.

We set up camp near the city of Hue. Everyone enjoyed the uneventful period; we cooked hot meals using empty magazine boxes and wood gathered from the nearby mountain. We picked edible vegetation to cook and made soup with fish scooped up from river after throwing grenades in it. I was amazed by how good the soup tasted with a pack of instant noodle added to it.

I continued to have nightmares, waking up at night with flashbacks of the horrible scene of the intense gunfire and the dead bodies of my fellow soldiers, especially that of Trung with missing body parts. I didn't know it was PTSD (Post Traumatic Stress Disorder) until I came to America.

After about a month stationed behind the front line, Dad came through with a special permit from the general that granted me a discharge from the service. The official permanent discharge certificate still had to be formally completed in Saigon. With my discharge order in hand, the MPs drove me to the city of Da-Nang where my Dad was waiting.

"Dad, what are doing here?" my heart was pounding when I saw Dad.
"I finally got the general to approve your discharge paper," Dad said with a big smile on his face. "Boy, am I glad to see you."
"I am so happy to see you, Dad."
"All right, let's get out of here!" Dad looked at me and still smiling.
"I don't have anything to take with me."
"It doesn't matter," Dad shook his head. "We can shop for anything you need."

We had a long hug with tears of joy streaking down our cheeks. I couldn't describe how happy I was to see him. Dad spent most of his time in getting the early discharge paper for me from the day I was wrongly detained by the Vietnamese police. I knew he would come through as he always had. He is my hero, and I owe him my life.

"Let's go eat," Dad said in an upbeat tone.
The first thing that Dad did was take me to a BBQ restaurant where he ordered a large plate of thin-cut raw beef to cook on the tabletop grill. The enticing smell of meat cooking over wood charcoal made my mouth water while waiting for the meat to cook; Dad added two more plates of beef before I put down my chopsticks and stopped eating – that was probably the best meal of my life.

Dad flew back home while I stayed with a distant relative in Da-Nang waiting for the official paper work to go through. It was quite appropriate for the occasion when I heard the song *"Yellow River"* on the radio, which reflected what was happening to me – *"Put my gun down the war is won . . .Cannon fire lingers in my mind . . .I'm so glad that I'm still alive . . .Got my papers got my pay . . .I'm going back to the place I love . . ."* – I finally got back to Saigon in June of 1972.

The emotion of seeing Mom and my siblings when I walked through the door was overwhelming.

"We were worried sick about you," Mom said when I ran towards her opened arms.
I gave Mom a big, long hug and whispered in her ear, "I missed you so much!" Tears of joy welled up in my eyes. Mom couldn't hold back her emotion; her eyes watered and her lips trembled but the tears couldn't hide her joy in seeing me. She had been waiting for this moment since I left home a year and half ago.

Mom cooked many of my favorite dishes to welcome me home. My siblings were so excited to see me; we stayed up all night talking about things that had happened while I was gone. They kept asking about my near death experience and couldn't believe what I had gone through.

A good friend of Dad's who worked for the American Embassy got me a job in the telegram and telegraph unit. The unit was located on the first floor of the new Embassy building on Thong-Nhat Street. The French Embassy on its left was separated only by an 8-foot brick fence; the two embassies took up an entire city block from Thong-Nhat Street to Hai-Ba-Trung Street in the 1st Precinct of Saigon.

My job was sorting incoming telegrams and telegraphs and sending them upstairs via a suction vacuum tube. The noisy machine also spit out code cards that carried hidden messages with the little holes punched out by the machine; the message could be read by a special machine on the 3rd floor. I just had to make sure those messages were sent to the proper department as soon as they came in. It was a rather brainless job but I enjoyed the opportunity to work with my American colleagues and the privilege of working in the U.S. Embassy.

Working under such a secured place safely guarded by the U.S. Marines was the exact opposite of my experience in the war zone! I felt peaceful during this uneventful period, and the normal mundane day-to-day things actually helped alleviate the trauma I suffered from that tragic battle in one evening not so long ago.

Left to right: My brother Ken & David, my cousin Khang, and me.
Taken shortly after my discharge from the Army – July 1972.

Chapter 4

The LAO's Trucking Company

Dad finally got a break when he ran into a former business associates, Mr. Dang, from North Vietnam who was then the CEO of a newly established sweetened condensed milk factory named COSUVINA in Saigon – short for their Vietnamese name of Congty Sua Vietnam (the Milk Company of Vietnam) – under the license and supervision of the Dutch Longevity Brand from the Netherlands. Mr. Dang was familiar with our trucking company in North Vietnam. Dad got a contract from him to deliver finished products to the retailers and transport imported milk powder from the seaport of Saigon, as well as sugar from local factories (the two main ingredients for making sweetened condensed milk) to the milk factory in the city of Thu-Duc 30 miles north of Saigon.

"Don, we will meet with Mr. Dang this afternoon. I want you to come with me," Dad said.

We arrived at the elegant corporate office of COSUVINA with an appointment to see Mr. Dang.

When we walked into Mr. Dang's office, he came to the door to greet us.

"Hello, Alan. It's good to see you again. This is Mr. Si, our marketing manager. He oversees distribution of our products," Mr. Dang turned around to introduce Mr. Si who was standing behind him.

"How do you do, Mr. Si?" Dad walked up and shook Mr. Si's hand. Mr. Si was about Dad's age and wore thick glasses.

"How do you do?" Mr. Si responded with a smile.

"I would like you to meet my son, Don," Dad introduced me. "Don will be helping me with the trucking business."

"Hello. Have a seat, please." Mr. Si said to me.

"Good to meet you, Sir." I reached out and shook hands with them before sitting down.

"Alan, Mr. Si will be working with you and Don on the trucking related matter."

"Thanks again for giving us the opportunity."

"Don't mention it; we've known each other for so long," Mr. Dang continued. "Mr. Si has the agreement for you to sign; it's just a formality."

The trucks we brought from North Vietnam had been sold, so Dad made an arrangement with his friend who was running a trucking company to rent trucks from him. Dad also agreed to use his drivers and pay them salary. The former LAO's Trucking Company from North Vietnam was re-established. This marked the turning point of our lives in the South. I quit my job at the U.S. Embassy and got ready to assist Dad in running the trucking company.

I visited Mr. Si every afternoon to deliver signed receipts of the deliveries we had made and obtain shipping documents for the following day. I handled all the logistics – setting up schedules and assigning the proper number of laborers to each of the trucks. I did the bookkeeping and prepared invoices to collect delivery charges from Mr. Si.

We delivered finished products to retail stores for COSUVINA all over Saigon and cities nearby. Business was good and we made our first million Piasters within a year. In addition to the trucks we leased, we bought two of our own and continued to rent an additional four to eight more trucks depending on the delivery orders received. At our peak, we could have a fleet of up to 12 ten-ton trucks running all over town during the week. In order to facilitate easy loading and unloading, we used flatbed trucks exclusively.

Loading and unloading were done manually with Vietnamese laborers we hired; Vietnamese made up of 90% of the manual-labor market. These folks were from low-income neighborhoods and only had grade school educations. Because Chinese business owners treated them well and paid them fairly, they preferred working for Chinese companies. By nature, the Chinese are more aggressive in improving their lives so there weren't many Chinese laborers in Vietnam. Historically, the Vietnamese look up to the Chinese as a result of years of influence by this giant neighbor. The older generation of Vietnamese read and write Chinese. They also follow many Chinese traditions, including celebrating the same holidays.

The workers we hired were young hardworking men and women who made very little from loading the trucks as well as carrying cases and cases of condensed milk (forty-eight 14-oz cans per case) on their shoulders from the truck to the warehouse or storage area of retail stores. They also had to shoulder 80-pound bags of imported milk powder unloaded from the ship or 100-pound bags of sugar from the factory storage warehouse onto the truck, and unload them when we got to the milk factory in Thu-Duc.

During the week, my day started at 5:00 am. After a quick stop for breakfast, I would pick up the laborers with our van as I headed to work. I drove them up to the milk factory and gave them their assignments along with the drivers' schedule for the day. I would rendezvous with the trucks during the day to ensure the deliveries were properly made and to collect signed receipts.

When COSUVINA was asked to supply the Vietnamese Army with condensed milk, Mr. Si introduced me to Major Nhiem who was the Vietnamese officer in charge of the Army Depot. I noticed the forklifts in the Vietnamese Army Depot, and COSUVINA had several forklifts in their warehouse, so I suggested to Mr. Si that we should stack the condensed milk onto wooden pallets and use the forklifts for loading and unloading.

"I like the idea, Don," Mr. Si said. "Make the necessary arrangement with Major Nhiem and let me know if you need anything."

"Thank you!" I said to Mr. Si. "Can you give the factory staff a headsup and I will work with them on the details?"
"Absolutely!" Mr. Si said with a smile.

It was a smooth transition, with the agreement signed by Major Nhiem and the cooperation of the milk factory. After implementation of the new process, we cut the loading and unloading time for each truckload of 500 to 600 cases of condensed milk from two hours to twenty minutes. However, the laborers were not happy with the arrangement because they would not have the opportunity to work on shipments delivered to the Army depot. They threatened to strike. In order to avoid the delay in making deliveries, I quickly negotiated a deal with their leader to settle the dispute by offering a 10% pay increase for the work that required manual labor of loading and unloading of deliveries outside of the Army depot. I explained their demands to Mr. Si and received a fee adjustment to compensate for the extra cost; I was proud and excited to be able to come up with a win-win solution for everyone.

I became friends with Major Nhiem and we hung out after hours from time to time. He later bought a used truck and hired his brother as the driver to become part of our fleet. Major Nhiem was a well-educated man. He was tall and good-looking; he was also a soft-spoken guy. He invited me to his wedding in his hometown of Can-Tho, which is a couple of hours' drive from Saigon. It was a traditional Vietnamese wedding with the bride and groom dressed up in their traditional Vietnamese-style formal wear. The bride had a full-length gown that split at her hip with the front and back flowing over the white pants; her hair was wrapped with a headband made of red fabric that was almost an inch thick. The groom wore an elegant red jacket that looked like a Chinese martial art uniform with a tightly buttoned upright collar.

After the ceremony, there was a banquet for all the guests. I gave them a pair of gold bracelets as their wedding gifts and wished them well before driving back to Saigon.

ICCS

As part of the exit strategy, the U.S. government orchestrated the Paris treaty for a cease-fire between the North and the South, which was signed by all parties involved on January 23rd, 1973. The International Committee of Control and Supervision (ICCS) was established by the United Nations to oversee the carrying out of the peace agreement. In order to be fair to both North and South Vietnam, the ICCS was run by a committee composed of two free-world countries (Iran and Canada) and two communist countries (Hungary and Poland). Ambassadors from these four countries met every Friday to discuss and report on the implementation of the peace treaty to the United Nations, as well as the parties involved (North Vietnam, South Vietnam, the USA, Russia and China).

When I saw recruiting ads for an editor for the ICCS, I sent in an application just for fun. But to my surprise, they came to our house looking for me a few weeks later and asked me to come in for an interview.

During an extensive interview, the lady in charge asked, "Mr. Lao, have you been to the United States?"

"I have never been to the states, Madame."
"But you speak English like an American."
"Thank you. As stated in my resume, I am an English major and I had the opportunity to practice speaking English when I worked for the PX. I also took courses at the VAA," I explained.
"We would like to offer you the job, Mr. Lao."
"Wow! I don't know what to say, but I am running a family-owned trucking company," I responded. "I don't think I have time to take another full-time job."
"I hope you could consider our offer."

"I am really flattered. You are so kind," I responded in appreciation. "Thank you for the interview and I apologize for not being able to accept your offer."
"Why don't you think about it and give me a call next week?" she said.

They were so impressed with my English; they thought I attended college in the U.S. I turned down their offer and explained to them that I really did not have time to take on another job.

On September 20th, 1973, they convinced me to take the job by allowing me to work only one day a week, when the ambassadors had their weekly meeting on Fridays, with a handsome salary of 100,000 Vietnamese Piasters per month – approximately $1,000 US dollars – while the average salary of white-collar employees was 35,000 Piasters a month! They paid me in cash, so I got two stacks of 500-Piaster bills every month and gave them to Mom. Mom kept the money in her dresser as rainy-day funds; I noticed her comforting smile when she looked at the drawer full of cash. Dad put the profit from the trucking company in the bank.

The ICCS editing unit was run by a Canadian lady and three editors – a Vietnamese gentleman, an Englishman, and myself. We transcribed and edited the minutes of the ambassadors' meetings and sent the final version to the United Nations with a copy to all countries involved – United States, Russia, China, South Vietnam, North Vietnam, as well as the four countries that ran the ICCS (Iran, Canada, Poland and Hungary).

I was proud to have worked for this historic organization of the Vietnam War era, and the fact that I was able to help Dad run his trucking company at the same time. I thoroughly enjoyed working simultaneously on two rewarding jobs. The job often meant 12-16-hour workdays, but the work did not feel intense at all, just satisfying. I refined my English from working for the ICCS and learned how to manage people running the trucking company for Dad. The bookkeeping course I took with the University of Michigan gave me confidence to do the accounting for our trucking company. With such success at the age of 25, I felt like I was on top of the world!

Because of our business relationship with the COSUVINA Company and my daily interaction with Mr. Si, he and his wife became good friends of mine, and I was often invited to have dinner at their house. I could see that Mr. and Mrs. Si were impressed with my background of good education, my proficiency in English, my ability in running the trucking company, as well as the fact that I worked for the high-profile ICCS. Not only had I earned admiration and respect from Mr. Si and his staff, but my family was also proud of me. In fact, a lot of people thought highly of me just because I worked for an international organization involved in the history-making peace process of the Vietnam War.

I began to realize why Dad said education was important. He also said education is not just what we learn in school; we gain knowledge from every stage of our lives. I learned to speak good English from working at the PX and from listening to those great songs; I learned to treasure family relationships through all the things Dad did for me from the day I was forced to join the army; I learned about team work and true friendship serving in the Airborne Division with Trung; I learned how to work with people through Mr. Si and the folks working for our trucking company; I learned how to run a business from Dad; and my learning is always ongoing and never ending. Education not only improved my life, but it also made me a better person. Dad's wisdom and caring helped shape my life.

CAT and MOUSE

Although my discharge papers were duly signed by the proper official, my tip-top physical condition did not convince the police and MP's of the fact that I was no longer fit for military service. The fact that I am a Chinese did not help, either, because there was a certain level of prejudice against Chinese by the Vietnamese officials.

Corrupt policemen set-up surprise checkpoints and targeted draft dodgers in and around the city. They use these to blackmail young men of military age between 18 and 35, especially the Chinese, who were known to be easy targets for blackmailing. They would threaten overnight detention for "further clarification" and ask for cash in exchange for on-the-spot release – I vividly remembered what happened to me. The ransom could range from $5k to $20k Piasters each pop! In order to avoid these traps, I paid attention to what was ahead on the road and took alternate routes when I detected surprise checkpoints ahead. I even bought a military Jeep from an excess equipment auction by the government and styled the Jeep to look like the government vehicles that were rarely stopped by the cops.

Motorcycles were the most common means of transportation for the vast majority of people in Vietnam. Stopping young men riding motorcycles at any of the checkpoints was almost guaranteed; therefore, I had to use my Jeep exclusively when I went out in order to avoid running into these checkpoints.

A permanent checkpoint was set up along Highway One – the Bien-Hoa Highway – to screen all vehicles entering the city. Because the milk factory in the city of Thu-Duc was outside the Saigon city limit, I had to make the trip at least once a day to deliver shipping documents for our trucks before they could pick up finished product from the milk factory. On my return trips to the city, I always used the lanes reserved for military/government vehicles, which could make a slow drive through without stopping. Civilian vehicles had to stop for inspection, and occupants were subject to ID checks similar to border inspections by custom agents.

My brother David was with me one afternoon on our way to check on one of our trucks making a delivery near the Saigon Market. My Jeep was in service so I was driving our small pickup and didn't see the checkpoint around the corner. We were stopped and the cops wouldn't let me go, citing suspicion of the validity of my discharge papers. They asked for money. We went back and forth on the amount and finally reached a deal for an on-the-spot release of $20k Piasters in cash. I didn't have that kind of cash with me, so I had to send David home to get the money from Mom. Although I was furious about the blackmail, there was nothing I could have done to change their mind. David was disgusted with this whole scenario as well.

On a Friday morning when I approached the ICCS office to report to work, the road was closed with barricades and the area was heavily guarded by MPs and police. I hesitated for a moment and decided to take the risk of being detained by driving my Jeep right up to the barricade placed in the middle of the road.

"What can I do for you?" An MP walked up to the driver side of my Jeep and wanted to know my intention.

"I need to get to the office for a meeting," I pointed to the ICCS building office in the barricaded area and showed him my ICCS employee badge. After examining my badge, he signaled his partner, "Let him through." Whew! I got through without further questioning by the MPs, and I later found out that they closed the road to beef up security for the United Nation's envoy visiting the ICCS that day.

Moving to an upscale Condo

With the increased revenue from our trucking company, we moved to an upscale neighborhood in the city next to the well-known An-Dong Market in Cho-Lon. It was a two-story condo on the 3rd and 4th floors of a 30-unit building. Our new house came with the first refrigerator we had in South Vietnam (we had one when we were in North Vietnam). There was a master bedroom for Mom and Dad and two lofts on the lower level. Dad turned the larger loft into sleeping quarters for Bill, Tom, John and Bob, and Nora had the smaller loft to herself. We put bunk beds in the bedroom upstairs for David, Ken, Keith and me. The kitchen and bathroom were also on the 4th floor, with a small terrace we used to dry newly washed clothes. The vast majority of people in Vietnam did not have washers and driers; clothes had to be hand washed and dried on clotheslines.

An elementary school (Tze-Zung) for Nora, Bill, Tom and John was just across the street from our new condo. Ken and Keith went to a Chinese high school in the 5th precinct a few miles from our house, while Bob was lucky enough to go to the prestigious private English school that

I attended in the early 1960's – Khai-Tri English School. I used to pick Bob up from school in my Jeep.

Everyone agrees that Bob is the smartest one in our family; he was also a good-looking kid with big brown eyes. John was obedient and well behaved; he usually stayed up in the loft doing his homework when he got back from school and did not come down until dinnertime.

I was the oldest son, with an age difference of 22 years between Bob and me, so I was sort of the father figure for my younger siblings and I had shared the breadwinner responsibility with Dad since I graduated from school.

Tom was the easy-going one and he seldom got punished because he always had a light-up-the-room smile on his face. When I was home, I used to sit on the bottom step of the stairs reading the daily newspaper and Tom would sit next to me with his sweet smile, which brightened up my day and made all of my hard work for the family that much more worthwhile.

People say we all look alike except Bill, so we all tease him that he was adopted. Bill did well in school and always won an award for ranking in the top five of his class.

Although she was a very pretty girl, Nora was sort of a tomboy – no surprises here because she competed with her many brothers, and the fact that Chi was so much older than her. Nora was smart, competitive, energetic and a quick learner; she could get things done twice as fast. Nora was able to work her way to become the branch manager of the American First National Bank in Richardson, Texas.

Ken and Keith were very close, like Chi and me. They went to the same school and spent a lot of time together.

Chi got David a job at the PX after he graduated from high school. David later worked for Air-America – a CIA front that provided support for covert missions and supplies for air-crafts used by the CIA to fly support missions from the main Saigon airbase, Tan-Son-Nhat. David was in stock control responsible for filling orders and keeping up with the inventory. He didn't realize his job played a vital part in the CIA operation in Vietnam.

Following the drawdown of U.S. troops, the corrupt South Vietnamese officials were busy fleeing the country. The war lasted until April of 1975 when the North Vietnamese intensified the fighting despite vigorous protest by the free world, as well as the ICCS. The South Vietnamese forces were no match for the determined VC, and the U.S. was tired of fighting on their behalf. The South Vietnamese Government was dysfunctional; things continued to get worse and got out of control. The U.S. gave up on them and started evacuating essential agencies and personnel, along with troop withdrawal. An evacuation plan for civilians was also underway.

Vietnamese with ties to the U.S. government were given instructions to apply for evacuation permits, which would include their family members. Anyone who worked with the American or the South Vietnamese government would be a prime target for retaliation by the VC. The wealthy people paid large sums of money to leave the country because the Communists would take over their properties and wealth; their status as "capitalists" could also be a reason for detention.

The friend of Dad's who got me a job with the U.S. Embassy said he could secure an evacuation permit for me with my prior employment record with the U.S. Embassy. Dad discussed his offer with Mom and me.

"I think you should go with him because of your work history with the American Embassy, the PX and the ICCS," Dad said. "It wouldn't be safe for you to stick around."
Mom looked at me and added, "I agree. The fact that you served in the Airborne Division could mean trouble also."
"I don't know. What about you guys?" I hesitated. I was torn between the opportunity to go to America and leaving everyone behind.
"Don't worry. We will be fine," Dad tried to make me feel better.

Dad took me to the airport in my Jeep the next day, and we waited at the gate with his friend's family.

"Dad, your status as a business owner could be the target for them. I still don't feel right leaving you all behind."

"But this is an opportunity you don't want to miss."

"I know," I tried to reason with Dad. "But you also need help with the big family if they take everything from you."

"Dad, I want to go home," I said decisively after standing there quietly for a while with my mind running 100 miles per hour with all sort of scenarios.

"Okay, let's go home." I could see the relief in Dad's face; he obviously struggled with me leaving also.

We explained our decision to his friend and wished him well before we went home.

On April 25th, 1975, David received an evacuation permit from Air-America that allowed him to include his family members. However, there was an age limit on siblings over 16, which meant Ken, Keith and I were not eligible.

"I got the permit to take everyone except Don, Ken and Keith," David told us.

"All of us need to be together!" Dad quickly responded.

"Under the current situation, I don't think we have a choice," I added. "I can take care of Ken and Keith and keep the company going."

"No, people left behind in China in 1949 and North Vietnam in 1954 got trapped behind the iron curtain for years without the freedom to reunite with their families," Dad insisted. "I can't let that happen to you, Ken and Keith."

"We should be able to join the ICCS if final evacuation is indeed necessary," I said.

"I need to think about this." Dad was still not convinced.

We heard about people leaving the country every day. Businessmen are considered capitalists and are subject to re-education and confiscation of their property, so many business owners, including Mr. Dang and Mr.

Si, paid their own way to leave the country. There was a sense of urgency to make the hard choice of leaving the country.

"Dad, it's time to go," I urged him. "You would be in trouble if the VC are really here."
"I don't know." Dad couldn't get over the thought of leaving us behind. "With just Ken, Keith and me, it will be easier to find a way out than with the entire family," I tried to reason with him.

Our family seemed to be on a runaway rollercoaster. Since our relocation from North to South Vietnam, our lives had been full of turmoil and uncertainty. It seemed as if circumstances had just begun to improve when another crisis threatened to separate our family.

After further discussion with Mom, Dad reluctantly changed his mind and decided to take advantage of the offer from David's employer, the CIA. I knew it was a difficult decision for him particularly because it meant separating his family and leaving three sons behind. I shared the same feeling with him, and I respected his courage in doing what was best for the family under the circumstances.

Dad and Mom, along with David and my younger siblings, packed lightly with food prepared by Mom and got in the family van. I drove them to the Tan-Son-Nhat airbase and sent them off with mixed feelings. It was difficult for me to see them leave because my family had never been apart before. Now I realized how they felt when I was sent to combat; the fear of losing your loved ones was a difficult emotion to cope with. I wondered what would happen to my brothers and myself now that we were totally on our own.

My family left on April 28th, 1975 for Guam on a C-130 military transport plane operated by the American Air Force. They stayed in Guam for 10 days before they were transferred to a refugee camp in Fort Smith, Arkansas, which was a well-equipped facility that housed thousands of refugees. As new refugees continued to arrive, the camp was filled to capacity. Mom said when he heard of new refugees coming to Fort Smith, Dad would go to the entrance hoping to see Ken, Keith and me.

Even though he was disappointed time after time, Dad continued to watch for new arrivals at the gate until they left Arkansas.

Church groups and individuals around the country were very active in sponsoring families for resettlement in their respective states. They reviewed the background of the family before selecting them for an interview. The United Methodist Church of Dallas, Texas, interviewed David and my parents in July. Spearheading the sponsorship was Mr. and Mrs. Whitley who were active members of the church's charitable work. These generous people provided housing and food for the transition period. They also helped the refugee families with everything they needed, from shopping for groceries to finding jobs.

Under the leadership of Mr. and Mrs. Whitley, the United Methodist Church of Dallas decided to sponsor our family for resettlement in Dallas, Texas, in August of 1975. The church provided a fully furnished 3-bedroom house and made arrangements for my younger siblings to attend school. Mr. Whitley got David a job working in his auto part manufacturing plants in Garland, Texas. Dad helped out at the church with maintenance and the prep work for the Sunday sessions. Our family was lucky to be selected by the Whitleys, who will always have a special place in our hearts; we will always be thankful to these kind and generous folks.

Coming to America was a culture shock to Dad. He did not speak English, and the American lifestyle was totally foreign to him, but it was not the first time he moved to a new place. He said, however, the Whitleys and the good people from the church helped make the transition so much easier for him; they were there almost on a daily basis to attend to everything our family needed. David was the only one who spoke English at the time; he was a tremendous help to Mom and Dad as well as the younger siblings. Dad's excellent driving skills quickly earned him a Texas driver's license; he managed to get around and take Mom to shop for groceries without David's help. Meanwhile back in Vietnam, my brothers and I often talked about the rest of the family over dinner and wondered how everyone was coping with their new lives in the U.S.

Chi got married shortly after my return from military service in 1972 and gave birth to their son, Dennis, the following year. They moved to Taiwan prior to the fall of Saigon. Mom and Dad sponsored them for resettlement in Dallas in 1977.

Chapter 5
The Fall of Saigon

On April 30th, 1975 I saw from the third story balcony of our house South Vietnamese police and military personnel abandoning their uniforms and vehicles on the street. People were rushing onto the streets cheering and shouting, "It's over! It's over!" I knew something was terribly wrong, so I drove to the ICCS headquarters to find out what was going on. The whole place was deserted with documents scattered everywhere, and people started looting. I went up to the personnel office where the administrative clerks were handing out certificates of employment to ICCS employees along with IOUs for our salary for the month of April, as well as our severance pay guaranteed by the United Nations, which formed and operated the ICCS.

I was disappointed to find out that all foreign nationals had left the country the day before without giving notice to their employees. The only explanation I could come up with was that they were caught off guard by how quickly the VC was able to topple the South Vietnamese Regime, and they did not have time to inform us. I had hoped for evacuating with the ICCS when it was time to leave. Being left behind by the people I trusted, I felt betrayed and scared.

"I am afraid we are left behind," I rushed home and shared the bad news with Ken and Keith.

"What are we going to do now?" Ken asked.
"There is nothing we can do. We just have to wait and see what happens next," I tried to assure them that everything would be all right, but I knew the outlook did not look good. "I will do anything to get us out of here. Trust me!"

I still don't know the answer to this abandonment because I was not able to reach anyone at the United Nations despite repeated attempts made during all these years. I have been trying to redeem the IOUs from ICCS by writing the United Nations, seeking help from the State Department and State Representatives, but have not been successful in getting my paycheck that is 40+ years past due. I will continue to try and plan to donate the money to charity.

Certificate of Employment from ICCS

SECRETARIAT

INTERNATIONAL COMMISSION
OF CONTROL AND SUPERVISION

OFFICE OF THE DIRECTOR OF
PERSONNEL & LOGISTICS SERVICES

C E R T I F I C A T E

(Lao-Coc-Tong)

This is to certify that Mr. .... Lao Hung Hanh ....

worked from....20th Sept 1973....to.....30 April.....1975 for the ICCS

Secretariat to the International Commission of Control and Supervision

in Saigon as..Transcriber/Editor.

COL. STANISSLAW MILLER
Chief, Personnel Section

Giay nay duoc cap phat le chung nhan rang One, ...(Lao-Coc-Tong)
...Lao.Hung.Hanh...da phuc vu tu nay..20.-04-1975....den ngay...30-04-1975

1975 tai Phong Tong Thu Ky thuoc Uy Ban Quoc Te Kiem Soat va Giam Sat

tai Saigon, voi chuc vu..Transcriber/Editor.

IOU Issued by the ICCS

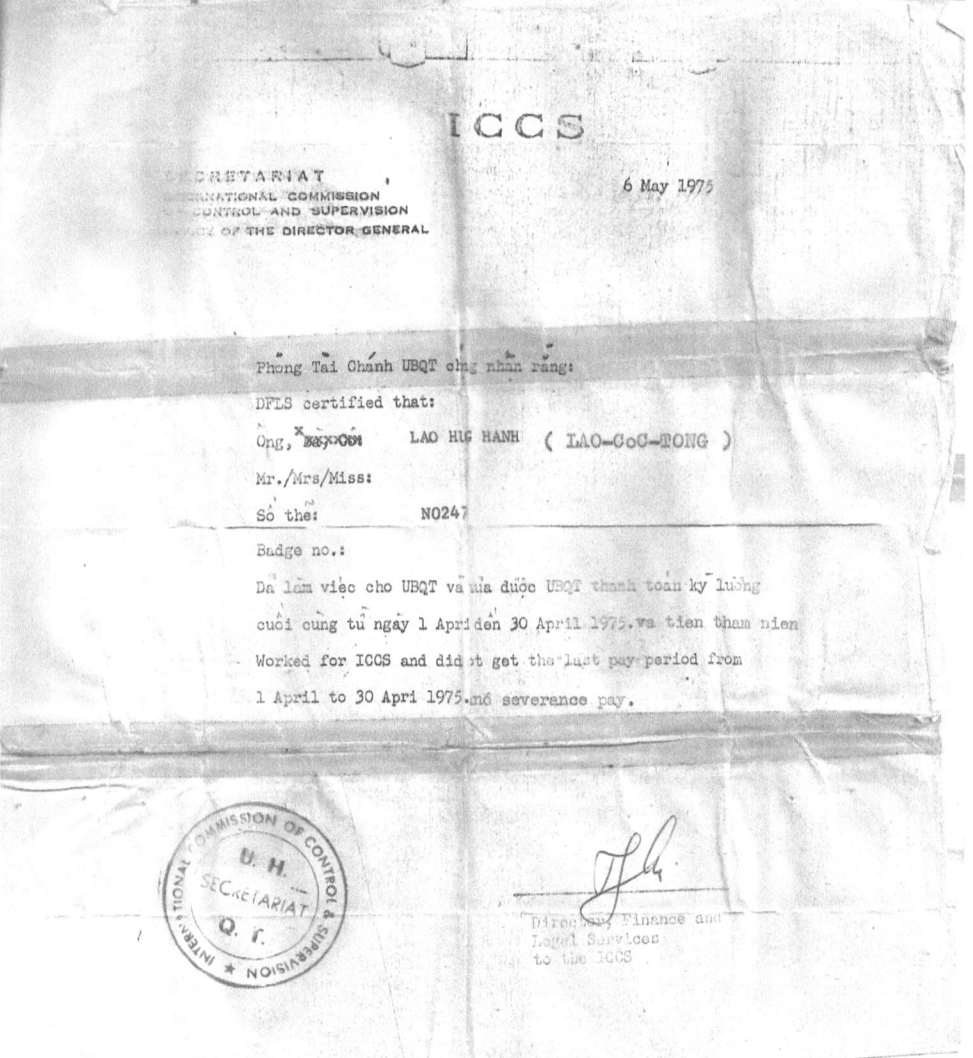

ICCS

SECRETARIAT
INTERNATIONAL COMMISSION
CONTROL AND SUPERVISION
OFFICE OF THE DIRECTOR GENERAL

6 May 1975

Phòng Tài Chánh UBQT chứng nhận rằng:

DFLS certified that:

Ông,   LAO HUG HANH   (LAO-CoC-TONG)

Mr./Mrs/Miss:

Số thẻ: N0247

Badge no.:

Đã làm việc cho UBQT và nửa được UBQT thanh toán kỳ lương

cuối cùng tử ngày 1 Apri đến 30 April 1975. và tiền thâm niên

Worked for ICCS and did t get the last pay period from

1 April to 30 Apri 1975. and severance pay.

Director, Finance and
Legal Services
to the ICCS

Prior to the fall of Saigon, the South Vietnamese forces, together with thousands of refugees, retreated from central highlands towards Saigon. Many of the evacuated soldiers had their families with them – one foreign news agency dubbed the mass exodus "the convoy of tears". Da-Nang and Cam Ranh Bay were captured; other smaller cities were quickly taken over by the North Vietnamese troops. They pushed south to the city of Bien-Hoa and turned the huge military base formerly built up by the American troops into their command center.

The whole invasion took less than a month. By the time they reached Saigon, the former South Vietnamese leaders had abandoned the presidential palace on Thong-Nhat Street. North Vietnamese tanks filled the streets of Saigon, and other provinces in the South surrendered without resistance. People were cheering on the streets. Looting, however, was not widespread for fear of retaliation by the unpredictable communist regime.

The working class had been fed up with the corruption and incompetent leaders of the former government; they felt "liberated". The poor also took the opportunity to vent their frustration from the struggle they had under the old regime by looting. Better-educated and well-off citizens were aware of the potential impact in a Communist society. Ethnic Chinese like our family would be the latter.

North Vietnamese soldiers in their traditional green uniform and green hat took over guarding the streets and served as traffic police. They, however, were well behaved and did not harass the South Vietnamese civilians. The transition was surprisingly smooth and uneventful for the victorious VC.

Up until the morning of April 30th, 1975, frantic Vietnamese with ties to the U.S. government gathered outside the U.S. embassy waiting for their turn to get to the rooftop helicopter to be ferried out to the awaiting military vessels. U.S. Marines keeping the crowd at bay were overwhelmed by the large number of people trying to get in. Foreigners had the priority to get through the tall iron-gate before any Vietnamese with evacuation permits were allowed to get inside.

With the order to move out, the remaining marines who retreated to a waiting helicopter on the roof for the last flight dropped tear-gas grenades to prevent people from coming up. The desperate crowd broke down the gate and looted the embassy building; that last helicopter flight marked the end of the American involvement in Vietnam.

The port of Saigon was virtually empty with ships and boats taken by people to leave the country; abandoned cars and motorcycles left behind by them were everywhere. Markets and shops were closed, and public transportation was halted with government offices abandoned. The once busy streets were littered with items left behind by the looters. It was the political vacuum period with no law enforcement. The chaotic period lasted only a couple of weeks, and things gradually got back to normal with the presence of North Vietnamese troops.

Prominent people who had worked for the Americans were arrested, along with former South Vietnamese officers, and sent to labor camps. The fear of their rounding up business owners for re-education did not occur, but the communists were known to be unpredictable.

With most of the records destroyed by the Americans before leaving Vietnam, it would not be easy for the VC to trace my employment history with the American Embassy and the PX; however, I would have to wait and see what could happen to me as a result of my taking over the trucking business from Dad. Although I could argue my service with the Airborne Division was involuntary, I was still uncertain about my fate.

It was estimated that 150,000 to 200,000 political prisoners were kept in two types of camps – one for long-term incarceration and one from which releases were made periodically after "successful re-education". It was speculated that these prisoners lived under poor conditions with just enough food to survive; many became ill or died inside the camps. For fear of being detained, many tried to flee by boats, which started the waves of boat people leaving the country illegally.

No one could imagine the entire country was deserted by the South Vietnamese government in such a short period of time. People were still scrambling to find boats and any watercraft that could take them out to sea, hoping to be rescued by the U.S. Navy. People still remembered the closing of the iron curtain in 1954, when anyone who did not leave North Vietnam was trapped under the communist ruling for 20 years! I kept the thought of not being able to reunite with our parents to myself because I didn't want to panic Ken and Keith. I did, however, assure them that I was committed to finding a way for us to leave at all costs.

I was saddened by the news of Major Nhiem being sent to re-education camp after the fall of Saigon and I never heard from him again. I was not sure what exactly happened to him, but I suspected a life sentence of hard labor because he was a high-ranking officer of the South Vietnamese Army.

I went to the office of COSUVINA (the milk company we did business with) and found the remaining staff frightened and in disbelief about the drastic change. Everyone seemed to be stunned and was unable to comprehend the magnitude of what had just occurred – the entire government was displaced and temporary ruling was taken over by the North Vietnamese military officials. Each company was assigned a leading officer who had to authorize any major business decision.

Col. Hien was the officer assigned to run COSUVINA; he was in his late 50's – a soft-spoken chain smoker who was trying to get his arm around a major corporation of the city. With no business background, he relied on Mr. Huong, a former V.P. of COSUVINA, to assist him with the duties of a CEO.

Mr. Huong introduced me to Col. Hung and we got along quite well in carrying on our trucking business with COSUVINA. Instead of Mr. Si prior to the fall of Saigon, I began having business meetings with Mr. Huong and Col. Hien and developed a good relationship with them. Although I did not have much dealing with Mr. Huong, I had seen him in the office from time to time. I had reservations about this strange relationship, and I was not sure I could trust them. I kept reminding myself to tread carefully in dealing with these people.

I often had dinner with Col. Hien at Mr. Huong's house on Le-Loi Street and played card games after dinner. I could sense that they liked me, and the respect was mutual. I bought gifts for Col. Hien during traditional Vietnamese holidays and on his birthdays. Mr. Huong was a smart guy; he understood his loyalty to Col. Hien would give him a safe shelter from being prosecuted for his status as a former capitalist. Loyalty of the South Vietnamese to the new government was superficial, and their motivations were self-serving – Mr. Huong was a classic example.

April 30th became "the liberation day" to the Vietnamese people. There were traitors who spied on people and turned on those who did not follow the communist agenda. These spies were known as "30's" as the fall of Saigon occurred on the 30th of April.

CONFISCATION OF PROPERTIES

"This is it," I said to myself when I received a notice from the local authority to make myself available for an interview regarding our trucking company and our properties.
"My fate will soon be determined," I shared my thoughts with Ken and Keith.
"What should we do?" Ken asked.
"There is nothing we can do at this point. Let's wait and see how it turns out, but I will take full responsibility and leave you two out of it," I said firmly.

An officer and his staff came to our house, taking inventory of everything under my father's name, including three 10-ton cargo trucks and my Jeep. They froze Dad's bank account, although it did not have a lot of money left. We had already taken money out in anticipation of the VC taking over.

I was instructed to deliver the trucks and the Jeep to a nearby location within a week.

After reviewing the ownership documents, the officer said, "Everything seems to be in order. You need to bring the trucks and the Jeep to this address tomorrow."

"Yes, Sir." I nodded.

"Fill them up before you deliver them to us," he reminded me repeatedly.

"I will." I couldn't believe I had to fill up the vehicles that were taken away from our family! It just irked me.

"Because you have been cooperating with the authority in preserving the national properties, we will grant you the permission to stay in this house," he added.

"Thank you, Sir!" I responded quickly.

I told our drivers to prep the trucks to come with me the following day and I drove the Jeep myself to the designated location. It was an abandoned warehouse with an office by the entrance.

"Sir, I have the order to bring in these vehicles," I showed the guard the documents.

"Park over there and see the officer inside," he pointed to the parking area in front of the warehouse.

"Over here!" I signaled the drivers behind me.

I turned in the keys along with the order I brought with me.

"Mr. Lao, you are free to go since everything is under your father's name," the officer in charge said after I had signed the "donation" papers. Ken and Keith were relieved when I got home and told them what happened.

With just the three of us boys left, the house felt empty and lonely. Mindful of the ongoing war, Mom kept a good stock of food and rice because we had a big family; we still had five 100-kg bags of rice in the kitchen and a freezer full of food she bought. I did some cooking in the beginning, but we ended up eating out most of the time.

I hired a lady to cook and do house work for us after a few weeks. She was a good cook and did a great job in keeping things neat and clean around the house, including washing and ironing our clothes. I paid her a monthly salary and asked her to eat with us, but she opted to save a portion for herself and ate after we had our meals.

In order to maintain our trucking contract with COSUVINA, I made arrangements to rent from individual truck owners/operators. I reserved only three trucks because production at the milk factory was reduced to one-third of capacity due to the low inventory of imported milk powder left over from prior to the fall of Saigon; import of raw materials was also greatly reduced with so many issues the new government had to deal with. Without renewed supply of raw materials, things went from a bustling industrial environment to a snail's pace, with most of the businesses shutting down or at reduced capacity.

In order to keep our trucks from idling, I sent them to bring bananas from farms in central Vietnam back to Saigon for wholesale. I leased a place for storage and distribution near the Saigon Market with Ken and Keith taking turns manning it. Ken and Keith often brought three to four-foot bunches of good quality bananas home and hung them in the kitchen for our own consumption. Kids in our neighborhood were allowed to come to our house and have free bananas whenever they wanted, so we had kids gathering at our house all the time. It was a much needed distraction with so much on my mind.

As a way to take my mind off things, I also took the neighbor's kids out for ice cream and held Christmas parties for them at our place. I cooked fried chicken and pasta for their Christmas dinner and decorated the house in honor of the occasion. They all got a bag of candies and cookies after dinner as a Christmas gift; Ken, Keith and I had a great time with them – I think we missed having our younger siblings around.

As the pace of production picked up, I shut down the banana wholesale business. I continued to make money from the trucking business and brought three used trucks and a VW van. Col. Hien awarded me with an exclusive contract that guaranteed ample business for our trucks, and I continued to rent additional trucks to meet the need. Despite the increased business and steady income, I did not feel good about our future under the communist regime, which was known to make unannounced changes to their policies overnight.

Schools were shut down, so I took Ken and Keith with me to help with the trucking business and keep them occupied. They rode with the truck drivers and collected signed delivery documents. When we had the banana wholesale business for six months, Ken and Keith were also busy in making the sales. They reacted well and seemed to be interested in taking on some of the responsibilities in running our family business. The new role was actually refreshing for Ken and Keith, and I believed the challenge helped them take their minds off thinking about our separation from Mom and Dad.

People were surprisingly adaptive and moved on with their new lives – they had no choice under the circumstances. Workers were forced to participate in the communist-style propaganda meetings everyday, singing and chanting, "Long live uncle Ho! Long live uncle Ho!" The Vietnamese communists worshipped Ho-Chi-Minh, and they addressed him as Uncle Ho. He was the leader of the Vietnamese Communist party before he passed away. The Chinese were known to distance themselves from politics. My brothers were too young to understand the impact Ho-Chi-Minh had on his country. I had heard of him and admired his devotion, but I did not believe Communism he brought to Vietnam was in the best interest of their people. What he did for his country was not important to me because I considered myself as a foreigner doing business in Vietnam. There was no future for me here. My family had already left, so I had no reason to stay.

Office workers were sent to join the blue-collar employees in daily exercise in the morning and then they worked in the fields once a week growing vegetables. It was really counter productive to ask office workers to work the fields, but it was just for show and the new government's way of flexing its muscle. Youth groups were organized to promote teamwork and a healthy lifestyle with weekly sporting events. A ping-pong table was set up outside the supply room of the COSUVINA office where the employees played and competed on a regular basis. I was invited to join as a guest player, and I brought Ken and Keith to play along from time to time.

MY FIRST DATE

Yen worked in the accounting department of COSUVINA. She was tall and pretty and I had been paying attention to her when I was working with Mr. Si prior to the fall of Saigon. With a reduced workload and a lot of time on my hands, I began my courtship by asking Yen out. We had our first date at a well-known floating restaurant by the Saigon River – Ben-Bach-Dang. I took Yen fishing and on short road-trips. We both liked to try new food, so we ate at different restaurants when we went out. Saigon was a modern city with many types of restaurants, so we were able to sample different cuisines. We liked lobsters and steaks at French restaurants; authentic Vietnamese dishes at Vietnamese restaurants; dim-sum and different types of noodle soup at Cantonese restaurants; and ice cream shops that also served freshly baked cookies. Yen was pleasant and smart; she had beautiful eyes and long hair. She likes to travel and enjoys seeing movies, which are also my hobbies. Because Yen worked for COSUVINA, it gave me the opportunity to see her every day during the week. On the weekends, we usually caught a movie after dinner if we didn't have a short trip planned.

The Change of Currency

The new government suddenly announced replacement of the South Vietnamese currency. Every family was instructed to report to the assigned location with the cash they had. Without prior announcement, each family received only $200 of the new currency that was equivalent to $100,000 Dong (the old Vietnamese Piaster) regardless of how much cash they brought in. All deposits in banks or financial institutions were frozen and seized by the government.

Fortunately there was a leak about the change of currency prior to this drastic move so everyone bought as much gold or American dollars as they could. I was able to secure 75 Taels of gold and $3,000 U.S. Dollars with the old currency I had. A tael of gold in Southeast Asia comes in the form of two and a half sheets of three-by-one inch rectangular thin sheet of gold leaf that weighs exactly one ounce, wrapped in yellow waxed paper.

$50 new currency (an equivalent of $25,000 Piasters) became the standard of monthly salary for everyone regardless of what position they held within an organization since everything was owned by the government.

With TV and radio stations taken over and tightly controlled by the communist regime, foreign radio broadcasts by the BBC, Voice of America and Radio Australia filled the gaps for people on what was really happening outside of Vietnam, especially the status of refugees, as well as the fate of those risking their lives on small boats to flee the country.

Family restaurants set up in front of their houses popped up everywhere as people were trying to generate income any way they could. The new government continued to dig up records of people with ties to the American and the former South Vietnamese government and sent them to re-education/labor camps. Fearing retaliation, people were looking for ways to leave the country. With the long coastline and numerous fishing vessels, fleeing by boat was the obvious choice. Failed attempts meant loss of lives and savings wiped out, but waves of people continued to try in their efforts to escape. Reports of overcrowded boats sinking were frequently heard while successful trips were few and far between. The entire family of a friend of mine lost their lives along with 300 other people onboard a small boat heading towards Thailand.

Because it was illegal to leave the county, finding the right contact to buy a seaworthy boat with a capable captain was extremely risky. The deal was usually made through a middleman, but an honest real deal was hard to come by. Many families lost their life savings to scams or got caught prior to boarding the boat. The market price was between 10 to 12 taels of gold per person – cash not accepted. Gold was the only form of payment for the illegal transactions, and gold could only be acquired through the black market with cash.

Chapter 6

Our Escape Plans

Mail service in Vietnam was finally resumed on a limited basis with mail delivery twice a week, but outgoing mail to foreign countries had to be taken to the only post office in the 1st precinct. We were ecstatic when we received a letter from Dad telling us about our family status and how they got to Texas for resettlement. David also sent us photos of everyone in the family, including a picture of the first car he bought (a Ford Mustang). I quickly reported our status to them. Although the snail mail was our only form of communication, it helped ease the pain of being apart. Knowing my family was safe and well taken care of, I began to direct my focus on how to get us out of Vietnam to reunite with them.

Similar to the Berlin Wall of Germany and the De-Militarized Zone (DMZ) between North and South Korea, the DMZ at 17th parallel separated the North and South Vietnam. Since the North and South Vietnam reunification became a reality, pre-war barricades, minefields and guard towers on both sides of the 17th Parallel were removed, allowing citizens to travel freely to either side of the country. Crowds of citizens from both sides crossed the DMZ in a celebratory atmosphere. People who had friends and relatives in North Vietnam went back to see them for the first time. Their visit confirmed our suspicion of the fate of "capitalists" after we left; businesses were taken over by the government and everything was rationed.

In contrast with the prosperous South Vietnam, the standard of living in North Vietnam had seen little improvement since 1954. With the help and support of the United States, South Vietnam experienced a rapid growth of their economy under a capitalist society. Citizens of South Vietnam were able to live well, enjoy the luxury of modern technology, own personal vehicles, and travel freely. Nearly the opposite was true in North Vietnam. Under the direct influence of the Soviet Union and Mainland China, its economy dragged and individual freedoms were severely restricted. There were a lot more pre-war buildings in North Vietnam; some still show signs of wartime damage. Bicycles were still the popular means of transportation; all automobiles were government owned and operated. Contact with the outside world was limited to a handful of Communist countries. The vast difference between the North and South Vietnam mirrored the situation of today's North and South Korea.

Since reunification, the new government has spent vast amount of resources in reintegrating the two halves of the country and bringing services and infrastructure in North Vietnam up to the level established in the south.

We were fortunate that Grandpa and Dad had the foresight to leave in 1954, and Dad made the right decision to evacuate with David to the U.S. in 1975. It was my turn to find a way out as soon as possible, and I was determined to follow Dad's footsteps.

The Balloon Project

While waiting for a load of condensed milk to be off-loaded from one of our flat bed trucks, I laid on top of the boxes soaking in sunrays and noticed the flowing of clouds from west to east. I came up with a crazy idea of building a balloon and riding the wind towards the Pacific Ocean from one of the coastal cities as an escape plan. We would then be picked up by ocean-going freighters or reach the Philippines as a way to join our family in the U.S.A.

Before I shared my plan with Ken and Keith, I invited cousin Khang over to include him in our discussion. They looked at me in disbelief when I told them about my idea.

"Are you sure?" Khang thought I was joking.
"I believe it's doable, but we need to do a little research to figure out what we need and how much it would cost," I responded enthusiastically.
"I agree with the research and planning," Ken said.
"I have no objection. Just let me know what to do," Keith added.
"Khang, please go to the library and bookstores to gather information. Ken, Keith and I will come up with a shopping list," I said to the group. They nodded.

After we had done our research and figured out what we needed for this wild attempt to flee the country, we began by ordering a wicker basket that was big enough to carry the four of us, as well as a supply of food and water. We built the balloon with materials from old parachutes and glued on nylon lining to make it airtight. Khang pointed out the opening of a hot-air balloon from a book he bought, but we did not know how to build the hot-air producing unit. We decided to go with the plan to get nitrogen/helium from a supplier in town.

For an ideal launch-site, I bought a piece of farmland a mile from the coast near the coastal city of Vung-Tau, 50 miles east of Saigon. We built a large launch pad in the back of the farmhouse with a 12-foot fence around it so no one could see the activities from the outside.

When everything was ready, we drove up to the site the night before and planned a midnight launch to avoid being noticed and shot down by the communist soldiers. We aired up the balloon after dark, but when it was fully inflated, it could only lift one person with limited supplies because the balloon was too small. After a long debate, we decided to abort this crazy attempt instead of sending one person off on this high-risk journey.

In retrospect, building a hot-air balloon, instead of our choice of a helium balloon, would have been much cheaper and more practical. A hot-air balloon would be much easier to navigate and control, and we would have had a far better chance to succeed.

With the failed attempt of my balloon project, I redirected my focus to finding a fishing boat like everyone else – fleeing the country was always on my mind because I didn't know what would happen to us under the unpredictable communist regime.

A distant relative hooked us up with a guy from Phan-Thiet, a coastal town in central Vietnam. We worked out the agreement and began planning our trip. Aunt Le-Quan and her four sons wanted to join us; so did my brother-in-law and Ken's girlfriend. Including the middleman and the fisherman's family and crew, we had a total of 20 people planning to set sail on a small fishing boat off the coast of Phan-Thiet. I did not include cousin Khang because we didn't have sufficient funds to cover him.

"I have a favor to ask and would like to keep this between us," I said to our neighbor and shared my upcoming plan with him.

"What can I do for you?" he was a little surprised.
"Because you are someone I know I can trust, I would like you to drive us to Phan-Thiet and I will sign over the VW van to you for your trouble," I explained.
Without hesitation he said, "I'll be glad to help." He was a trustworthy man that our family had known for many years.
"I have reserved a hotel room for you the night we get there," I added. "Wait until the following day before you go back to Saigon in case we need you."
"No problem," he said.

In order to blend in with the fishing villagers, we dressed down for the trip of our lives. It was quiet on our way up as everyone was nervous. We arrived in the evening; it was a bit windy, but there was no storm in the forecast. We got out of the van quickly and, our contact led the way through the village towards the dock. I noticed something wrong from the strange looks of those villagers along the way. Before we went any further, I stopped the group and told them to go back to the drop-off point.

"I have a bad feeling about this. I think we've been detected. We need to get back to town," I shared my thoughts with the group.
They agreed.
"It would be easier for me to get the car and meet you all there," I whispered to the group. "Spread out and avoid drawing attention."
They nodded.
I ran back to the roadside and paid a villager to take me on the back of his motorcycle to the hotel where my neighbor parked the VW van.

"Let's go! I will drive," I got my neighbor out of his hotel room in a hurry and drove like crazy towards the rendezvous point. When I got back to the village, I found our group sitting by the roadside surrounded by the North Vietnamese soldiers pointing AK-47's at them! I made eye contact with Yen and my brothers and slowly drove past before stopping further down the road. Seeing my loved ones at gunpoint, I was sick to my stomach and my heart was racing; I couldn't breathe and my head was spinning. This was my second PTSD episode, which still gives me nightmares of being caught along with my loved ones and incarcerated by the communist soldiers.

I went into town the next day and found out where the group was being held. It was a makeshift prison of two barn-like structures with corrugated metal roofs and sheets of metal with small holes as the sidings. There was one for male prisoners and another one for females. The area was fenced off with barbed wire and a guarded gate in front. I approached the guard and got his permission to send our group food, so I stayed for the next few days making daily deliveries before heading back to Saigon to figure things out. The situation couldn't have been worse!

I informed Yen's parents and Aunt Le-Quan's husband of the bad news, but I didn't have the heart to let Mom and Dad know – there was nothing they could do anyway, and I didn't want to worry them. Yen later told me that they were fed with the worst kind of rice that was not even clean (it had bits and pieces of rocks in it); she cried holding the bowl of rice that she usually wouldn't touch, but she was too hungry not to eat. Yen said there were no walls or dividers inside; holes on the metal siding served as ventilation and light source with no electricity. Over a 100 people shared the entire wood floor as their bed; they were packed like sardines.

Prisoners were only allowed to take baths once a week. Everyone had to get a bucket of water from the well. They were sent to the bathroom together in groups of males, then groups of females. The bathroom was made out of a 12'x12' rectangular metal shipping container with windows cut out on the side and an entrance in the back.

It was too hot to stay inside the metal structure under the grueling sun; they gathered and ate their meals in an empty dirt field. During the day, women had to work in the kitchen and pull weeds while male prisoners had to do manual labor around the camp. They were put back in the makeshift prison after dinner, and the guard chained up the doors and locked them inside until the next day. Each day to them was as long as a month. I felt so sorry for Yen and my brothers who had never gone through something this harsh in their lives. Yen still has nightmares about this horrific experience and swore that she would never set foot in Vietnam ever again. I shared the same feeling with my PTSD of this horrific experience. Ken, Keith and the boys were in the same situation, but they were able to mingle with the rest of the group during the day.

I went up to visit them on a weekly basis while trying to get them released. Despite numerous requests, I was not able to get anywhere. After a month, the VC captured another group of people trying to escape, so they let some of the earlier detainees go because they were running out of room. Yen and Ken's girlfriend were among the lucky few that were released. By the second month, the boys under 18 from our group were set free. Ken was just over 18, so he was retained for another month. I was so relieved and excited to finally have everyone home. I treated them with a well-deserved vacation to the resort town of Dalat for a week shortly thereafter.

Dalat was just thirty miles from Da-Rang, where Dad used to work for the Japanese building the hydropower plant, so we drove to Da-Rang and revisited the place we used to live. The housing unit was abandoned after the Japanese left. I couldn't believe how small our house was and wondered how everyone was able to fit into that small space. The infamous Japanese bathhouse was still there, but the interior had been torn to pieces by vandals. The mountain behind the house was as green as ever; it brought back a lot of fond childhood memories. We took a quick tour of the dam where we used to fish; it was quiet and peaceful. We drove down to the valley and took pictures of the hydropower plant, which was heavily guarded by the communist soldiers.

Ken and Keith's Journey to Thailand

Instead of putting all eggs in one basket, I began planning another boat trip just for Ken and Keith. I would be the home base providing support and serving as the point of communication between them and my parents in the U.S. A friend of mine hooked me up with a middleman who had planned a successful escape for his family members, so I knew I could trust this source. The price was 10 taels of gold per person and it had to be paid in advance. I had no choice but to make the payment of 20 taels of gold with my friend as the only witness to this under-the-table transaction.

I got the green light from the people that organized the escape for Ken and Keith on March 28th, 1977. They arranged a bus ride for Ken and Keith from Saigon to the coastal city of Ha-Tien, which is located at the southern most point of Vietnam bordering Cambodia. It is the closest point to Thailand by boat.

Ken, Keith and I had a long talk the night before their trip. I made sure they understood the plan and reminded them to stay alert and watch out for each other. They dressed down to look like teenagers from a fishing village returning home with bicycle parts purchased in Saigon, and I drove them to the long-distance bus station the following day. We met with the contact person at a coffee shop next to the bus station; he went over the travel plan with us before Ken and Keith got on the bus with him.

After the bus took off, I left with a lot on my mind, wondering if I had made the right move. How could I face Mom and Dad if anything happened to Ken and Keith, and how could I live with myself, for that matter? On the other hand many people are taking the same risk for freedom, I thought, so I had to make this difficult decision as Dad did in 1975!

I struggled with the mixed feelings and couldn't sleep until I received word from our contact a couple of weeks later that Ken and Keith had safely arrived in Thailand. The good news was confirmed by a telegram from Mom and Dad in Garland, Texas when the Thailand refugee camp officials notified them of Ken and Keith's arrival. When I walked out of the post office with the telegram, I ran straight to my car and buried my head on the steering wheel. My heart was racing and I yelled, "Yes! Yes! We did it! Ken and Keith made it!" The load on my shoulders for the past two long weeks was finally lifted with this great news. Fearing that the VC might be suspicious of the whereabouts of my brothers, I couldn't share the good news with anyone but Yen. I took Yen to dinner to celebrate that evening.

I knew Ken and Keith would watch out for each other during their time in the refugee camp in Thailand until they reunited with Mom and Dad in the U.S.

Here is Keith's account of the journey of their lifetime:

On March 29th, 1978 brother Don drove Ken and me to the long-distance bus station and we met with the contact person who made arrangement for our trip. He gave us the bus ticket and explained the detail of our travel plan. He instructed us to follow him discreetly and not to talk to him during the entire trip. He said he would be sitting right behind us and his presence was to ensure our safe arrival. In order to make sure we were not being followed, he said there would be a total of three different leaders assigned to escort us. Each leader would take turn in watching out for us, and the change of guard would occur at a major bus stop. So our full cooperation was critical.

We waived good-bye to Don with a heavy heart when our bus took off. The bus made quite a few stops before we reached Ha-Tien late in the evening. I noticed a total of three rotations of the leader sitting behind us until we reached our destination.

"We'll get off here," the man assigned to escort us whispered from behind; his presence was to ensure our safe arrival and we know where to get off. We followed him to a waiting car.
"Let's go," he instructed the driver after we got into the car.
They took us to a small farmhouse and offered us food and drink.
"Wait for me here," he said as he left the house. "I will be back shortly."
Six other boys our age were brought in shortly after our arrival. The man came back after dark and led us to the beach.
He told us to lay low and said, "I can only take two at a time. You all have to be quiet."
It took him more than an hour to transport eight of us (two at a time) with that small canoe to a tiny island off the coast. We walked up to a straw hut behind the coconut trees where there were already a dozen young men sitting there; we were the second group to arrive.
"Stay here with them. We have another group arriving tomorrow," the man said before he left. He continued transporting new arrivals to this rendezvous spot until the final count reached 32 young men; each of us paid 10 taels of gold for this journey to freedom.

After a couple of days hiding on the island, the man came back and told us the third group would not be joining us because one of the boys dozed off on the bus and forgot to get off. He and a few of the people traveling with him were detected and detained by the VC. It was a terrifying reminder of how risky our trip was.

The man was supposed to bring our carrying bags that had a few essential items and change of clothes we brought with us, but the mishap of the 3rd group forced him to speed up the process, and he was not able to retrieve our bags before we boarded the fishing boat for our trip. We had to walk from the farmhouse to the boat anchored off the shore, so he told us to leave our shoes behind. The fishing boat for our journey to Thailand was no longer than 30 feet that had just enough room for the passengers and a crewmember.

The skipper stood by the small doorway hustling us under the deck where we were packed like sardines. We slept sitting up and leaning against the side of the boat. The air was filled with smells of sweat and body odor.

I fell asleep while the boat continued to move away from land. When I woke up the next day, we were in the middle of the ocean with nothing around us.

The skipper allowed us to come up to the deck for fresh air. But he would not allow everyone to come up the same time in order to keep the boat bottom-heavy for fear of tipping over.

It was dark after sunset, and we were drawn to the sky filled with bright stars in the glow of moonlight.

"Why are we not moving?" someone asked.

"I have good news and bad news," the skipper said. "We have reached international water, so we are no longer in the VC territory."

"The bad news is I have never been sailing this far and I don't have the equipment to set the right course for this boat at night," he continued. "In order to make sure we are heading west towards Thailand, I have to rely on the sun to set the right course."

"Oh my God. Is this how he navigates?" I said to Ken.

"It would be safer this way," the skipper assured us.

So we went through the routine of drifting at night and sailing during the day. April usually has no stormy weather in the Gulf of Thailand, so many people chose this time of year to sail. We barely had enough to eat but fortunately there was sufficient drinking water onboard.

The vast ocean connecting to the sky at the distance looked incredibly beautiful and captivating during the day. We were excited to see fish swimming along our boat, especially the dolphins. The louder we cheered them on, the harder they swam.

We were all alone in the ocean for the first couple of days, but we began sighting other fishing boats in the distance on the 3rd day. We got close to one and shouted out to them for help, but they sped away seeing a group of shirtless young men waiving and yelling at them. We had not taken a bath since we left Saigon and didn't have clothes with us to change; what we had on was all we had. They must have mistaken us for pirates with so many people getting robbed on their way from Vietnam to Thailand.

We finally got the attention of a Thai fishing boat; they gave us food and pointed out the directions to Thailand. We reached a small fishing village that evening. Curious Thai residents of the village gathered at the dock asking questions while we were still on the boat. When they found out that we came from Vietnam and ran out of food, they gave us crackers and some kind of Thai soda and said we had to sail on further to reach the Chanthaburi Refugee Camp. It was not much, but their generosity warmed our hearts.

We continued to sail along the coastline and arrived at the Ko-Kut Island of Thailand on the 5th day. The Thai residents on the island treated us with food and drink. They gave us clothes and we had our first bath since we left Vietnam. They told us we were close to our destination, Chanthaburi Refugee Camp, which was just a couple of days away. After feeding us and helping us replenish supply of food and water, they sent us off and wished us good luck. The arrivals of refugees had become a routine for them.

We stopped at the Ko-Chang Island on the following day, and we were treated with the same hospitality we received in Ko-Kut. Ko-Chang is a much bigger island with nice houses along the beach.

"These must be wealthy people's vacation homes," I said to Ken.
"You!" A Thai girl pointed at me and signaled me to come to her and offered me the pineapple that she just cut up.

When she saw insect bites on my arm, she got a tube of Thai ointment from the house and said, "Put this on."
The good people of Ko-Chang gave us bread and fresh fruits, and some of residents volunteered to cook for us. After we were well fed, they offered a place for us to take shower (we had not taken a bath since we left Saigon). Mr. Hong, a Chinese on the island, stayed to talk to us and brought supplies that would last until we reach our final destination.

We had a good night sleep on our boat and woke up to a noisy crowd gathering at the dock. They brought us more food and supplies and freshly baked bread. Mr. Hong also came back with a whole case of fresh pineapples to send us off. The police chief of the island offered to lead us to the Chantaburi Refugee Camp – the closest Thai refugee camp near the border of Cambodia. He said we should be able to reach our destination by the end of the day. We waved good-bye to the generous people of Ko-Chang. Everyone was in good spirit with the heartwarming treatment we received, and we wasted no time to follow the police chief's boat to Chantaburi.

"Thailand! Thailand!" we all stood up and yelled.
As we approached the dock, we saw people gathering.
"We made it!" we said to each other and slapped a high-five.
We reached the shore of Chantaburi after 8 days riding the ocean waves from Vietnam in a small boat that was not ocean-worthy, piloted by an inexperienced skipper.

The Thai officials of Chantaburi apparently had seen frequent arrivals of refugees; they were not surprised to see us. They talked to us briefly and told us to wait at the dock. It was their tactic to make some money under the table by prolonging the waiting time. Our skipper seemed to have heard of the "custom" and knew exactly what to do. He slipped the officer-in-charge a few taels of gold from his share of payment he received for helping with our escape from Vietnam. A bus was quickly radioed in to take us to the refugee camp.

When we walked through the camp gate, a crowd of refugees gathered around us.

"Where are you all from? Saigon or the lower-six provinces?" people from the crowd approached our group and asked about the status of folks in Vietnam. Vietnam's coastal provinces near Cambodia and the Gulf of Thailand are referred to as the lower-six provinces.

"Get back!" An officer yelled at the gathering crowd and lined us up for the registration process. It took a while before Ken and I had the opportunity to provide personal information and answered questions about our escape. After we had filled out the required forms, we were sent to a reception area to receive clean clothes, towels, toiletry items, and a light blanket. The clothes given to us were left behind by refugees who had left the camp for resettlement in other countries. They put us in a building for temporary shelter. We had a good night sleep after enjoying the shower we hadn't had for a few days.

There were approximately 1,500 refugees in this camp; we did not know who built those straw huts in the camp where the refugees stayed, but they had to be paid for by the refugees with gold or cash. Ken and I and six other boys pooled our cash together and bought one from a group of refugees who were leaving for resettlement in Australia in a few days. The hut was supported by wood posts with the floor elevated about four feet above the ground; it was just a 20'x20' empty shell with a stove set up as the cooking area in one corner. The rough wooden plank floor was where we ate and slept.

The man in charge said he sent a telegram to our Dad with the address we provided in the questionnaire. The workers told refugees without relatives in foreign countries it could take up to a year to be sponsored by organizations or church group from those countries. We thought it would be quicker for us with Mom and Dad in the United States. All we could do was waiting for the paperwork to go through.

We waited in line every day for rationed food, water and other supplies. People with money could ask the workers to purchase things from the market for them; we bought meat and other snacks with money sent by Dad from the U.S. There was nothing to do other than wait and check on our immigration status. When there were new arrivals, we would stand with the crowd by the entrance hoping to see our brother, Don.

The hot and humid weather of Thailand made our days of waiting seem longer and longer. We arrived in April; May and June had come and gone, but there were still no words from the office about our immigration status.

"We are going to America!" I screamed when I saw our names on the newly published list on July 16th, 1978. Our official departure date was July 23rd. The thought of being able to reunite with our family in a week made us extraordinarily happy. We shared the good news with people we knew; they all congratulated us with admiration. We left everything we had with the remaining group, including a couple of hundred dollars of money order received from Dad earlier that week.

A bus took us, along with other refugees scheduled to leave the same day, to an apartment adjacent to the Bangkok International Airport where we received our immigration papers and waited a week for our flight.

After the check-in process was completed, we boarded the chartered flight arranged by the U.S. government. The thirty-something-hour flight took us to Houston, Texas, with a stopover in Paris. We flew to Dallas the following morning where Mom, Dad, David and the rest of the gang were there to greet us. It was an incredible moment hugging each and every one of them after such a long separation. I noticed tears of joy in Mom's eyes, and Dad couldn't stop smiling.

"I am finally free!" I uttered with joy and mixed emotion because I knew everyone had brother Don on their mind, wondering when would he be joining us.

Chapter 7

I Became The Boat People

Of the 300,000 people who left by boat from Vietnam, about 100,000 got to Hong-Kong; the remaining 200,000 chose the sea route heading south from Vietnam to Thailand, Malaysia, Singapore, Indonesia and the Philippines. Virtually all of them were residents of South Vietnam; the vast majority of them were Chinese. Ethnic Chinese were keenly aware of their fate under the communist regime with the perceived status of capitalists, and many of them had family members who had left Vietnam prior to the fall of Saigon. Vietnamese fleeing the country were those who had ties to the U.S. or the former South Vietnamese government.

These people traveled by small fishing boats paid for by the occupants with gold. For them, the shortest sea crossing was from coastal cities along Vietnam's Mekong River delta to Thailand or Malaysia. From the fishing port of Ha-Tien or Rach-Gia on South Vietnam's coastline to Malaysia is about 500 kilometers by sea; from the city of My-Tho or Vung-Tau near the capital of Saigon, it is about 750 kilometers. Reaching the northeast coast of Thailand was quicker and easier.

Many South Vietnamese residents had their minds set on fleeing the country to re-unite with their loved ones that evacuated prior to the fall of Saigon. The middlemen and boat owners benefited from the wealth of those people who paid them with their life-savings in the form of gold. Illegal attempts to flee the country were secretly arranged through the black market using gold as the form of payment, usually 10 to 12 taels of gold per adult (children would be half the cost) to finance the acquisition of a boat and related fees and commissions. Fuel and supplies essential for the life-risking voyage had to be purchased at inflated costs through the black market.

The new regime soon realized they would not have these people's hearts and loyalty. In order to capitalize on this opportunity to get rid of these unwanted citizens while gaining from the wealth of these desperate people, the Vietnamese authority appointed officials to organize the unofficial exodus. They set up registration sites in major cities, openly signing up families who wanted to leave; however, their offices were seldom located in government buildings. Their staff was in civilian clothes and the program was not advertised in the media, but spread merely by word of mouth. The controlled exodus spurred the growth of busy boat repair and construction on state-owned or state-approved shipyards.

The vast majority of the boat people leaving through the "assisted passage" channel were Chinese from around Ho-Chi-Minh City (formerly Saigon) and Cho-Lon, Saigon's China Town. They followed the black-market fare of 12 taels of gold for adults and half for children aged from five to fifteen; children under five with traveling adults were free. About half of the money went to the government, and the other half went to purchasing boats, supplies and fees for the middlemen.

Initially, ethnic Chinese in the South were skeptical of the semi-official program for fear of a trap. With reports of successful arrivals heard on the BBC and telegrams from friends who took the risk to leave, waves of people swarmed the registration offices.

Due to the high demand, the Vietnamese authority contracted with captains of small ocean-going freighters from Singapore and Thailand on route to Hong-Kong or Taiwan to provide higher capacity without having to retrofit or build small boats. The attraction of the freighters was that they were safer and faster, minimizing the dangers of piracy and death at sea.

The use of cargo ships gave the whole exodus a higher profile and led to the exposure of the trafficking of refugees. Voyages of the **Hai-Wan**, the **Huey-Fong**, and the **Sky-Luck** freighters exposed the program at its worst, with large number of refugees packed into unhealthy and unsafe conditions on small freighters that were ill equipped to handle these vulnerable passengers.

The difference between the exodus from the South and that from the North was that people paid their way to cross into China by land, starting in March 1978. The land route cost less than a third compared to the voyage by sea. The wave of refugees accelerated through July before China announced closures of its frontier with Vietnam. Peking claimed that China's southern provinces had accepted 160,000 ethnic Chinese from Vietnam. Because the cost was much cheaper going the China route, working class from the South also took the journey north, including many friends and distant relatives of ours.

The increasing numbers of refugees from Indo-china as well as from Mainland China brought to the attention of the Hong-Kong authorities the potential magnitude of the crisis. During 1979, 68,748 Vietnamese arrived in Hong-Kong.

Hong-Kong received the largest number of refugees than any other southeastern country – 68,748 in 1979 alone, compared with 53,996 by Malaysia, 48,651 by Indonesia, 11,928 by Thailand, 7,281 by the Philippines, and 5,451 by Singapore[3].

After Ken and Keith left, I knew I couldn't leave the country without Yen because I was so much in love with her. I proposed during an outing with Yen and she agreed to marry me. We got married in 1978.

---

[3]   From The Book *"Boat People"*

My cousin Khang and a few good friends of mine helped with planning the wedding. It was a simple reception with Khang as my best man. We invited close relatives and friends to the wedding party at a well-known restaurant in Chinatown. I was so happy that night; I got drunk and had to be taken home by Khang.

Yen's father came from Shanghai; he started working for the French Embassy in the early 1940's and worked his way to become the supervisor of the property and lived within the compound of the French Embassy in Saigon. Yen has two brothers and a sister. They lived at the Embassy from the time they were born until they left Vietnam. The French Ambassador had agreed to assist with getting Yen's family out of Vietnam, but he was not able to provide a set date for departure. As Yen's husband, I was also on their list for evacuation. Although Yen's Dad didn't speak Cantonese and I couldn't understand his Shanghainese, I could feel his warmth and affection when I was with him. Yen served as our interpreter when we were together. Yen's Mom is a Cantonese; she and I got along really well.

While waiting impatiently for the French Embassy's process to go through, a good friend of mine (An-Phi) informed me of his decision to go with the semi-official registration to leave the country via ocean-going freighters. An-Phi was a sales associate of COSUVINA; he and I had been friends since we started our trucking contract with the company.

"My neighbor who worked at the registration office assured me this is a legitimate program aiming to gain from the wealth of the Chinese," An-Phi said.
"I am still not sure. This is just too good to be true," I was still skeptical because of the incident in Phan-Thiet where we got caught.
"Here's his name and the office location if you change your mind."
An-Phi's family was the first group to sign up; they boarded the **Hai-Wan** freighter and arrived in Malaysia in the summer of 1978 as broadcasted on BBC radio.

With the assurance of the safe arrival of the refugees on the **Hai-Wan** freighter, Yen and I registered in September of 1978 and paid 12 taels of gold each. We received notification to leave in December, along with instructions on how to prepare for the trip as well as the gathering location thirty miles north of Saigon.

They only allowed a small carry-on bag per person, and we were not permitted to bring cash or valuable items, otherwise they would be confiscated. People hid gold and cash by sewing secret pockets inside the liner of their jackets, inside the hems of their pants and women's bras. We followed the method to hide the couple of hundred dollars we had; we didn't have any gold left.

Prior to taking the trip, I destroyed all documents and photos that we were not able to take with us. I was not able to assign our house to anyone because it was in Dad's name; however, the contents not physically attached to the house could be removed, so I asked Ping to take everything the day before my departure. She rented a truck and emptied the house, including food items in our refrigerator. With limited income and no savings, her family was not able to afford to leave Vietnam. She was in tears when I gave her the goodbye hug; it was an emotional moment for me to leave this sister of mine.

I told my cousin Khang that we were leaving and asked him to drive us to the gathering point the following day.

"Can you take us there?"
"Absolutely. What time should we leave in the morning?"
"No later than eight."

We arrived at the designated location in the morning and presented our proof of registration to the guard at the gate.
"Check their bags and take them to the waiting area," the guard said to one of his helpers.
"Follow me," the man said after a quick check of the two carrying bags that we had. We followed the instructions to bring only clothes, two light jackets, some food, and toiletry items.

We walked to an open field where families signed up to leave huddled in groups. We found an empty spot and sat down as well.

The buses finally showed up later that afternoon. We lined up and boarded in groups. A ferry docked at The Saigon River (Ben-Bach-Dang) was waiting to take us up river to the port of Vung-Tau, fifty miles southeast of Saigon, where we were escorted to the 2300-ton **Huey-Fong** freighter. Before the ship got to Vietnam, it was fully loaded with cargo picked up in Bangkok for delivery to Taiwan. They struck a deal with the Vietnamese officials to make this unscheduled stop to pick up refugees in exchange for gold.

Our group had around 800 people; everyone fought for a good location on the deck for their family as the small living quarters were only reserved for the crewmembers. The hull was filled with cargo, so only the upper deck had room for these unscheduled passengers. With no one directing where we should go, people grabbed the best spot available for their families. The crewmembers, not used to handling such a situation were overwhelmed by the large number of refugees.

As the first group to board, I was lucky enough to secure a spot behind the navigation bridge for Yen and myself. Yen was two months pregnant by this time. The walkway where we stayed was about eight feet wide. The bridge behind us and the overhang above provided shelter and some privacy. Yen slept on the floor, and I hung a hammock between two posts overlooking the deck below for me to rest. We had the corner next to the access door to the crew's cabin with five other families to our left; the bed sheets we spread over the wood floor defined each family's spot. Our limited belongings were placed within the space of a twin bed and the bags of clothes served as our pillows. People huddled together to keep warm at night; no one was complaining knowing it was only a temporary situation.

"Why is the ship still not moving?" Yen asked after everyone had boarded.
"I don't know. Let me see what I can find out," I began to worry and went down to the deck below.

A group of refugees were asking the same question and gathered around to discuss it.

"Do you all know what's going on?" I asked them.

"No, we are wondering why we are still here," one of them responded.

"Let's find out," I suggested.

We tracked down one of the crew members and asked, "Mister, why are we not leaving?"

"A second group will be joining us tomorrow," he said in the lowest possible voice.

After a second group of people came onboard, the ship was still docked portside the next day. All sorts of scenarios were running through my mind, and I rounded up the group of men I talked to yesterday and suggested that we pay the captain a visit. They agreed and we went to the bridge.

"Captain, can we talk to you for a second?" I asked the man in uniform.

"What can I do for you? I am the second officer of the ship," the guy manning the bridge responded.

"Why are we still here?" I questioned impatiently.

"We have to wait for the clearance for departure," he explained. "But we should be able to set sail for Hong-Kong tomorrow."

A third group of people got on board the third day before our ship was cleared to depart. We later found out that the final count of refugees on board this tiny cargo ship was 3,186. As seen in the photos taken by reporters, the ship was packed with refugees. Every inch of the deck was taken with people jammed together like sardines all the way to the railing. Refugees from the final boarding group had to go to the front section of the deck, which was filled with people all the way to the bow and exposed to the elements.

As we were about to leave the port of Vung-Tau on December 13th, 1978, two Vietnamese gunboats followed us at high speed. My heart lurched to my throat.

"My Lord, we are caught again and will be put in jail," I said to myself and nervously watched our ship slowing down.

When the gunboats caught up with us, they signaled our ship to stop. "Drop the ladder!" the VC holding an AK-47 shouted into a bullhorn. The crew followed his order and lowered the ladder on the side of the ship. We saw a small group of 10 civilians lined up single file and climbed up under the watchful eyes of the VC. After signaling us to sail on, the gunboats sped away as fast as they came.

These people paid the local coastguards with gold as the bribe for taking them to our ship; they were the final few to board. Our journey finally began and the feeling of seeing Vietnam behind us was indescribable; Yen broke into tears of joy – we were finally free! I felt the anxiety and worries I had were lifted off my shoulder at that moment.

I looked at the land behind us with mixed feelings. While I was overjoyed to be finally on my way to reunite with my family, the sadness of leaving a place I called home for the past thirty years was overwhelming. Vietnam was where my family endured two evacuations and three decades of war. In addition to serving in the South Vietnamese Army, my family owned a business and I had worked for the PX; therefore, I had three strikes against me for being detained. The strong possibility of being sent to a re-education camp kept me searching for a way out since the fall of Saigon. For fear of being punished as capitalists, my Dad gave up everything in 1954 to move south, and it was déjà vu all over again. Although I knew I was at the beginning of another difficult journey to rebuild our lives, I had no regrets because I was hopeful about the new opportunities available in America.

We ran into rough seas the first night and the ship was rocking back and forth violently, but it seemed to be holding up quite well with the weight of the cargo and passengers. We found out a child died during that night; the captain held a brief ceremony the next morning and buried the child at sea.

While we were at sea, everyone lined up for distribution of hot soup and congee, along with drinking water, twice a day. Makeshift toilets built with scrap wood from unused pallets and tarp hung along the side for privacy were set up along the edge of the ship.

Because of the unexpectedly large number of people, we ran out of rice after three days, so our meals were down to crackers and sardines when we arrived at Po-Toi (just outside of Hong Kong) the fourth day. I worried about the shortage of food and poor hygiene on board. Many people got sick. It was quite a contrast between the well-equipped and well-prepared American transport vessel that took us from North Vietnam to Saigon in 1954.

Because our spot was right behind the navigation bridge, the captain and his second mate saw Yen and me every time they passed by. They sympathized with Yen being pregnant in such a harsh condition; the second officer gave her bread and fruits from time to time.

"Thank you!" I said to him while nodding my head. He smiled.
"Put the bread away. We don't want other people to see," I warned Yen. I was thankful that Yen got something decent to eat while everyone onboard had only rationed crackers and sardines.

As our ship got near Hong-Kong, it was intercepted by the Hong-Kong coast guard and Royal Navy patrol boats. Our captain lied to the Hong-Kong authority and said that he and his crew rescued boatloads of refugees off the Vietnamese coast after discovering that they were running out of fuel and supplies. The authorities instructed our captain to maintain his course towards Taiwan and blocked our entry to the Hong-Kong harbor. Our Captain, Shu-Wen-Shin, slowed the ship down and we could see Hong-Kong at a distance to the left of our ship flanked by two fully armed patrol boats.

Our captain was determined to get the refugees ashore; he slowed the ship to a barely moving speed and surprised the Royal Navy by kicking into full gear and speeding past the patrol boats. He then made a 90-degree left turn heading straight towards the Hong-Kong harbor!

We were chased by the patrol boats with flashing lights and blaring sirens behind us. They finally caught up with us and blocked our ship from getting too close to the harbor, but our captain refused to leave and dropped his anchor. The ***Huey-Fong*** vessel became a floating refugee camp outside of the Hong-Kong harbor from that moment.

The Hong-Kong government started daily communication with our captain and agreed to provide drinking water and canned food to us. We ended up having crackers and sardines for a month and spent the Christmas of 1978 on the ship. We were confined to a small area and had nothing to do. Yen and I spent our days talking about our new lives in the U.S. and envisioning the happy moment of reuniting with our families. We talked about naming our child and the choice of color of our first car in the U.S.

While leaning against the railing of the upper deck, I spotted Yen's Aunt and her three kids on the front section of the deck below. They were the third group of refugees to get on board so they had to settle for a spot near the bow of the ship. With no empty space left, some of the refugees had to sleep on top of wooden crates stacked on the deck.

"Yen, your aunt and her kids are down there!" I ran back and told Yen.
"Where?" Yen came with me to the front railing of the bridge.
"Down there," I pointed at the bow of the ship.
"Go get them," Yen said excitedly.
I moved them up to our spot. They were extremely excited and thankful to run into us. The families to the left of us were kind enough to make room for us to accommodate this single mom and her three young kids. Her son, Kien, was nine, and her two daughters (Veronique and Pricilla) were 11 and 13, respectively.

When Kien got really sick on the ship, I asked the captain to radio in a medical emergency, and the Hong-Kong authority sent a helicopter to take him to the hospital. They flew him back to the ship after he got well a couple of days later. I still remember the smile on his face because the nurse gave him a big bag of candies and cookies to bring back to the ship.

We sought permission from our captain to form a refugee committee. With my multilingual ability in English, Vietnamese and Chinese (Mandarin and Cantonese), I served on the committee along with five other gentlemen. We met with the captain on a daily basis and communicated the progress of our negotiation with the Hong-Kong government to the refugees. We also discussed our plan of actions in getting the attention of the United Nations and other free-world countries, especially the U.S.

After a couple of days docking outside the Hong-Hong Harbor, boats with reporters from around the globe circled our ship, taking photos of the refugees onboard. Our committee crafted the wording for banners that we hung along the railing of our ship, urging the United Nations (UN) and the world to intervene on our behalf. We asked the refugees to hold up some of the banners and waive at the reporters; they screamed and jumped while the reporters were busy snapping photos. Because I speak fluent English, I served as our captain's interpreter, and I gained the trust and respect of our captain and his crew.

A reporter from the *Los Angeles Times* came over the radio of our ship and asked to speak to the refugees. Our captain put me on the two-way radio for an interview.

"Hello, who I am talking to?" the reporter asked.

"My name is Tong Lao. The captain asked me to speak on behalf of the refugees," I responded.
"Good. The captain said I need to be brief. Can you describe the conditions on the ship?"
"Children are malnourished and many people are getting sick because of the poor hygiene onboard. We have not had a hot meal for over a month," I began describing the situation onboard.
"How many refugees are on this ship?"
"3,186."
"Is everyone from Vietnam?"
"Yes, we are from Saigon."

I shared with him the shortage of food and the poor living conditions and pleaded for his help in getting the attention of the UN and the U.S. government.

After a thirty-minute conversation, he said, "Thank you," and asked if there was anything he could do for me in return.

"My Mom and Dad are in Texas. Are you able to connect me?"

"I'll try. What is your Dad's number?"

"Area code 214, and the number is 272-1942," I gave him Dad's number and waited on the line.

"It's ringing. The connection could only be a couple of minutes," he said in a hurry.

Dad was excited and surprised by the call and thought I had arrived at Dallas without giving him advance notice.

"Where are you?" Dad asked with curiosity.

I briefly explained where I was and asked him to plead with members of U.S. Congress and House of Representatives to intervene on our behalf so we could get ashore and begin the relocation process as soon as possible.

"It's great to know that you are okay," Dad said in a trembling voice.

"Tell Mom and everyone that Yen and I are fine." I responded quickly.

"We've got to go," the reporter interrupted.

"Dad, they are going to disconnect us," I quickly said to Dad. "I will call as soon as I have access to a phone."

"Take care of yourself," Dad said before the call was cut off.

"Thank you for helping me with the call," I said to the reporter with appreciation.

"Good luck to you, Mr. Lao."

A friend of mine later told me he saw this interview in the *L.A. Times*. I was proud to speak on behalf of the refugees and excited to be the only person on this ship to be able to make a phone call to the U.S. Being able to talk to Dad under the situation was unbelievable.

While we were waiting for the decision of the Hong-Kong government, I designed a registration form to capture pertinent information of each refugee family onboard. In addition to their name, age, and profession,

I had a "Remarks" section for them to indicate which country they preferred to take refuge in and to provide information on any of their relatives in that country. I numbered the families from 1 through over 600 for easy identification – Yen and I were #325, and her Aunt's family number was #326.

Negotiation with the Hong-Kong government went on and we finally had the attention of the United Nations (UN). We knew there was a breakthrough when representatives from the UN boarded our ship to meet with us. They informed us that the Hong-Kong government had agreed to provide us with temporary shelter while they worked with countries that would be willing to take refugees. They told us the process might take some time because of the number of refugees involved, but they were in awe when I handed them the completed family registration forms that had all the information they needed.

"You are very organized," the UN representative smiled while he took the stack of forms from me.
"It's our pleasure, Sir," I bowed and said. "Thank you for helping us."
"You are welcome," he said. "With the information you have gathered, the process shouldn't take too long."
With the UN intervention, the debarkation process started later that week.

The day before we were allowed to go ashore, the Hong-Kong authority airlifted to the ship our first hot meal of the month; the stewed chicken wings and steamed rice never tasted better. We all had a full meal and were ready to get off the ship.

The port authority gave instructions to our captain to dock the ship at the port of Kowloon. The screening process required us to go through a quarantine tent with medical staff dressed in white overalls and covered with masks spraying every refugee with some sort of chemical before we got to the security checkpoint. The last group of refugees went ashore on January 23rd, 1979 pending re-settlement overseas. 3,186 refugees were on the ship under unhealthy condition for over a month! Yen was in tears when we were about to get off the ship. I was thankful for a better environment for my mother-to-be wife and looking forward to getting the resettlement process started.

We were told that our captain and his crew were detained by the Hong-Kong police. A total of 3,500 taels of gold were discovered hidden in the engine room of the freighter. The captain and his crew were charged with conspiracy to defraud the Hong-Kong government by bringing refugees in illegally. A group of us petitioned for the release of Captain Shin and his crew, but we did not know the fate of these saviors of ours.

Hong-Kong was the home base of **Huey-Fong**, and the trial was the first court case to expose the organization behind the big-ship refugee racket.

After the **Huey-Fong**, a ship name **Sky-Luck**, a 3600-ton freighter, left Singapore on January 12th, 1979 with a cargo of paper and other merchandise. The five-day journey to Hong-Kong turned into 27 days because of the unscheduled stop in Vietnam to pick up 2,630 refugees registered with the Vietnamese officials who made the arrangement for the voyage.

Based on a United Nation figure as of July 1979, a total of 93,624 Vietnamese refugees resettled in various counties as follows[4]:

Australia = 17,571
Austria = 134
Belgium = 230
Brazil = 37
Canada = 7,428
Denmark = 270
France = 5,527
Germany = 2,595
Greece = 44
Hong Kong = 149
Israel = 188
Italy = 100

---

[4] From the book *"Boat People"*

Luxembourg = 45
Malaysia = 8
Netherlands = 290
New Zealand = 735
Norway = 799
Paraguay = 31
Sweden = 267
Switzerland = 875
UK = 2,505
U.S.A. = 53,815

Sadly, 81 refugees died before reaching the resettling countries according to the same United Nation report.

Chapter 8

Hong Kong Refugee Camp

We were taken to an abandoned military housing complex within the old Hong-Kong Kai-Tak airport. It was a six-story building with empty rooms on each floor and no furniture. Four families were assigned to a 30'x30' room; each family occupied a corner as their sleeping quarter. Yen and I were assigned to a room on the third floor with three other families.

A unit of Hong-Kong police was assigned to run this camp. Officer Tam was the man in charge. We lined up single file everyday for lunch and dinner with a stainless steel bowl in hand. When it was our turn, the guards filled our bowls with steamed rice and spooned the day's dish on top. We also had the choice of an apple or orange before settling down at an available spot on the lawn; early birds would be lucky to find a shady spot under the trees. We could hear the street traffic over the 16-foot concrete fence.

When Officer Tam learned that I was multilingual, he asked me to assist with putting up signage in the public area and bathrooms reminding everyone to maintain a clean and sanitary environment for the place we were going to be in for a while. This camp later served as a transitioning stop for new refugees when our group was moved to a more organized refugee camp in the Sham-Shui-Po district of Kowloon. Families with relatives or friends in Hong-Kong were allowed to live outside the camp, but they were required to report to the refugee camp on a weekly basis and check on their relocation status.

Uncle Wing and a close friend of ours, Mr. Si, the former marketing manager of COSUVINA, offered to take us in. Because Mr. Si owned two restaurants in Kowloon and asked me to assist with running one, we chose to stay with him.

Uncle Wing was okay with my decision. He and his wife took us to eat and sightsee when he had time on weekends. We enjoyed the food from different specialty restaurants; my favorite dish was the Sha-Tin roasted quail. This restaurant roasted the quail over natural wood charcoal, which gave the crispy skin a unique flavor along with their special seasoning. My mouth waters just from thinking about it. Uncle Wah and his wife also joined us on some of the outings.

Yen's Aunt was a life-long friend of Mrs. Si, so she and her children also moved in to stay with Mr. and Mrs. Si; her daughter Pricilla also helped out at Mr. Si's restaurant. They were later sponsored by a relative to resettle in San Francisco.

I made my weekly run to the camp checking on our immigration status to the U.S. By mid-1979, various countries had accepted the relocation of refugees and families began moving out of the camp to resettle permanently in their newly adopted countries. Listings of families and their final destinations were posted daily on the bulletin board of the camp's administrative office.

Yen gave birth to our child, Steven, on May 2nd, 1979 at the Caritas Hospital of Hong-Kong; he was a healthy baby weighing eight pounds. We shared the good news with my parents in Texas, and Yen's parents in San Francisco. The French Embassy had finally helped moved them to France shortly after we left Vietnam. They relocated to San Francisco in the spring of 1979 to live with Yen's older brother.

I continued to work at Mr. Si's restaurant until August of 1979 when our names were on the list for relocation to the U.S. with the sponsorship of my parents in Garland, Texas. Mr. Si arranged a farewell dinner prior to our departure and invited Uncle Wing and Uncle Wah to join us. The dinner was held at one of Mr. Si's restaurants; many special dishes were prepared for this special occasion. While I was excited and anxious to see my family in the U.S., I felt sad leaving a group of people who took care of us during this unusual time of my life. I took the opportunity to thank Mr. and Mrs. Si for their exceptional hospitality and friendship. I thanked Uncle Wing and Uncle Wah for spending time with us while we were in Hong-Kong. During the dinner, Mr. Si proposed a toast to wish us a safe trip and a good life in America.

The refugee relocation organization chartered a plane flown by American Airlines to bring our group of refugee families from Hong-Kong to the U.S. We had a stopover at Eielson Air Base near Fairbanks, Alaska, before landing at Davis Air Force Base in Northern California on August 30th, 1979.

We were taken by bus to San Francisco. That was the first time I was on the highway in America; the freeway was wide and each direction had its own separate lanes safely divided by concrete barriers. There was only a thirty-mile stretch of highway like this in South Vietnam; the remaining roadways were two-lane roads with only a yellow line in the middle as median.

This was the beautiful country that I had dreamed of seeing since I started working for the PX. Although everything looked so new to me, it did not seem foreign because I had studied the culture, the society, the food, as well as the lifestyle of this great country.

With anxiety and excitement, my eyes were glued to the captivating scenery.

"Is this the Golden Gate Bridge?" I asked the driver when we crossed the Bay Bridge.
"No, the Golden Gate Bridge is over there," he pointed to the right.

"Wow! It's beautiful." I saw the historic red bridge behind the magnificent skyline of downtown San Francisco.

"Yeah, it's the most popular landmark of San Francisco," the driver said proudly.

Arrangements were made for us to stay at the Travel Lodge adjacent to the San Francisco International Airport and board our flight the next morning for our journey to Texas. Yen's parents and her brothers and sister came to see us at the motel and held Steven for the first time before we headed to Texas the following day. All these years later and Yen and I can't stop looking at the Travel Lodge Motel every time we drive by on highway 101 from San Jose to San Francisco.

My family and Mr. and Mrs. Whitley, as well as a couple of church members (Paul and Pauline), came to the Dallas airport to welcome us. I ran over to give Mom and Dad a big hug when I saw them at the gate. I then introduced Yen to my parents and siblings. This was the very first time Yen had met my family with the exceptions of Ken and Keith. Yen handed Steven to my Mom who was thrilled to finally hold him in her arms.

David introduced the two couples to Yen and me. He said Paul and Pauline helped my younger siblings with homework during the initial period of resettlement in Dallas. Mr. Whitley was in his late 50's and wore glasses. He was short and chunky but looked respectable in his suit and tie. Mrs. Whitley was about his age but she was a little taller than he was. She wore a light-blue jacket over an elegant pink-and-white dress. Paul looked friendly with a big smile on his face. He was thin and tall and wore a pair of big, round glasses; he also dressed in suit and tie. His wife Pauline was slim and pretty. After shaking hand with them, Dad took a lot of pictures before we headed to the parking lot.

Mr. and Mrs. Whitley showed us their Cadillac Deville and said, "Don, this is America's most expensive luxury car."

"Wow, it's beautiful. It must be very comfortable," I inspected the limo-like car with admiration. "It looks like the President's motorcade I saw on TV."

"Yes, it's a privilege to own one," Mrs. Whitley said proudly.

Their pride of owning one inspired me to buy a Cadillac myself in 1988 – I got a brand new El Dorado coup.

Mr. and Mrs. Whitley were typical kind and generous Americans with good hearts. They lived in the upscale Parkland neighborhood of Dallas with their son and daughter. Mr. and Mrs. Whitley were board members of the United Methodist Church of Dallas, Texas, and actively participated in all of their charitable activities. They were the guardian angels of our family.

3613 LARIAT LANE, GARLAND TEXAS

With the help of Mr. Whitley, my parents bought a 4-bedroom house in Garland, Texas with a 30-year mortgage the year after their arrival in 1976. Everyone in our family will never forget the street number of our first house in the U.S. – 3613 on Lariat Lane in Garland, Texas.

Mom and Dad furnished one of the bedrooms with new furniture for the three of us, including a crib for Steven. Shortly after our arrival, Yen and Steven flew to San Francisco to spend time with her family while I tried to acclimate myself to my new home in Texas. David showed me around in his car, and I soaked in everything I read about when I was in Vietnam. My impression of this new country was exactly how I envisioned from my prior interaction with my American colleagues at the PX and the American TV shows of the 1960's that I fell in love with while I was in Vietnam. I was impressed with the well-paved roads as well as the cleanliness of streets and shops. Freeways full of vehicles were also new to me; it took me a while to get used to the high-speed driving. It was everything I had hoped for and so much more. No words could describe how good I felt.

There were not many Chinese in Dallas at the time, but we did not feel isolated or any tension living there because the people were kind and helpful. We didn't feel any prejudice, either. Dad found a small Asian grocery store near downtown Dallas, and we shopped there every weekend for Mom to cook authentic Chinese food.

MY FIRST JOB IN THE U.S.

In September 1979, David saw an ad by the Aetna Life & Casualty Company recruiting trainees to handle group health claims for Texas Instrument employees and urged me to apply. Impressed by the excellent benefits and extensive training program, I sent in my application and was hired shortly after an interview with their HR representatives. When David learned of additional openings, he also applied and was hired as well. It was late September, but we were told to start on October 15th at their office and the training facility in Arlington, Texas. I was proud to land a good job within a few weeks of my arrival in America; my obsession for learning English when I was in Vietnam paid off.

On the 3rd day of our arrival in the U.S., I took my driving test and got my Texas driver's license. With three weeks prior to starting our new jobs, David and I took the opportunity to make a road trip in his Mercury Cougar RX7 coup from Dallas to San Francisco for a visit with my in-laws. After 12 hours on the road from Dallas, we spent a night in El Paso before heading west through New Mexico and Arizona to California. Instead of Interstate 5, we took Highway 101 from Los Angeles to San Francisco so we did not arrive in San Francisco until mid-night. Not knowing the concept of credit card at the time, I thought David had a lot of money in the bank because he could get cash from ATM machines anywhere we went. I later learned that he was just drawing cash advances from his line of credit like many working Americans; this concept was totally foreign to me. Coming from Vietnam, the U.S. seemed so much more advanced in every imaginable way. People here enjoyed life while making a living was the focus in Vietnam. I felt so lucky to be an American.

We stayed at Yen's brother John's apartment in Mountainville, California and visited Yen's sister Christine and her husband in San Francisco. They took us sightseeing in and around San Francisco. We saw the Golden Gate Park, Fisherman's Wharf, Lombard Street, Union Square and Chinatown. David and I were also treated to excellent Chinese food and dim sum in San Francisco. Christine's husband drove us to the infamous twin-peaks of San Francisco one evening, and we ran into heavy fog on our way back, which made the trip even more exciting. I thoroughly enjoyed the opportunity to visit this world-class city that I could only read about in Vietnam. There were only a handful of nice buildings in the financial district of Saigon, and they were no more than five stories tall. Skyscrapers are common sites in every major city in America, especially San Francisco, Los Angeles and New York City.

We spent a week and a half with Yen's family before tracing our way back to Texas. It was my first road trip in America; the world-class roadways and the ease of long-distant traveling with gas stations and motels readily available made driving around the country a breeze. I thoroughly enjoyed it. Making a road trip of more than 100 miles in Vietnam was a major undertaking. Cars were old and not well maintained. An oil change was the only thing commonly done; cars were only taken to repair shops when they were broken. Well-paved roads and gas stations were few and far between; all major highways had only two lanes for two-way traffic with only a yellow line in the middle as the median. I remember having a 200-gallon drum in the back of my car filled with gasoline for our 300-kilometer trip from Saigon to Da-Lat.

AETNA LIFE AND CASUALTY COMPANY

When David and I reported to work on October 15, 1979, we were greeted by Ms. Lee O'Hara, the designated trainer. Our group of 10 trainees gathered at a meeting room for the daily lecture, and Lee went over the manuals and training materials with us. She was an excellent teacher and explained everything in a logical way. I took the training as my advanced education, so I paid close attention to everything Lee said and absorbed it like I was taking college courses. She also trained us on computerized claim processing; it was the first time I was exposed to a personal computer.

After six long months of training, we were assigned to a unit under Supervisor Lou Flatman. We had our own computer, which was used to process claims that we had reviewed. We issued checks electronically through the same computer at our workstation. Lou was pleased with our unit's performance and Lee was also happy to see the fruit of her labor. These two classy ladies as well as the trainees in our class became good friends of ours – David and I were the only two male employees in our unit; we were also the only Chinese in the entire office. As with the folks in our neighborhood, the people at work treated us as one of their own, without prejudice. I truly felt I was part of the office staff and enjoyed good relationships with my colleagues.

When we were not packing lunches for work, David and I went to the Church's Fried Chicken. The southern fried chicken I liked so much at the PX commissary was now readily available for me to sample anytime I wanted! Sometimes I thought I was still dreaming.

David and I took LBJ Freeway from Garland to Arlington to work everyday. At the LBJ Greenville street exit on our way back, we saw an Aetna sign so we inquired about a transfer for a much shorter commute. The long drive from Garland to Arlington (40 miles one way) had worn us out after a year and a half. I remember one morning after a snowstorm it took us three hours to get to the Arlington office. Lou laughed at us and said, "You two should have stayed home! Haha."

As American immigrants, we were tenacious, diligent, and hardworking in an effort to rebuild our lives. There was so much to look forward to; we were just happy to be accepted by this great country. The feeling of freedom and being worry-free could be experienced just by sitting at a Sonic Drive-In having a hotdog or hamburger while listening to classic oldies being played.

Initially, David and I drove his Lincoln Mercury Cougar to work. I received $750 in aid from the refugee assistance center for purchase of a car, so we used the money as down payment on a new Pontiac Sunbird in 1979. We took that car to work because it got better gas mileage than the Cougar with a V-8 engine.

My entry-level salary after tax barely covered our daily expenses. In order to supplement the income, I took a part-time job with the Target store in the Valley View shopping area. On our way home from the office in Arlington, David dropped me off at the Target store where I worked until 10:00 p.m. three days a week as a sales associate in the sporting goods department. My employee discount allowed me to get baby formula for Steven at a lower price.

With strong endorsement from our manger and supervisor in Arlington, David and I were offered a job with Aetna's Casualty Division in Dallas – the drive was only 20 minutes from our house in Garland, instead of an hour to Arlington.

David and I were later promoted to claim representative positions and were sent to the Aetna Home Office in Hartford, Connecticut, for further training in handling property & casualty claims, an entirely different discipline of claim handling from the group health operation in Arlington, Texas.

Aetna Life and Casualty Insurance Company was a first class company with offices across the country. We were treated with respect and dignity from day one.

Chapter 9

The Great Wall Restaurant

Mom worked part time as a cook for a Chinese fast food restaurant (China Bell) in the Valley View Mall of Dallas. Dad liked the simple business concept that could be managed by a family like us, and the owner of China Bell made good money during summer and holiday seasons when the mall was busy.

Knowing Dad's wish for having a restaurant of his own, I got in touch with the management staff of Richardson Square Mall in Richardson, Texas, for the possibility of building a similar fast food restaurant there. A friend of ours hooked me up with Watson Restaurant Supply Company in Dallas to provide equipment, as well as a general contractor for construction of the restaurant. I signed a contract with the Richardson Square Mall in 1981 and began building my parents' dream.

In addition to the equity of Dad's house, I also applied for a small business loan from the Commerce Bank of Richardson to fund this endeavor. With the equipment and construction loan covered by Watson Equipment Company of Dallas, the total cost of building this restaurant was approximately $100,000.

As with malls across the country, each store has a number and ours was #325 – the same refugee family number assigned to us on the **Huey-Fong**! Our home phone number was also (214) 245-0325. A coincidence or was it meant to be?

We named the restaurant "Great Wall" to signify an authentic Chinese restaurant and began construction in the spring of 1981. Unfortunately Dad had a heart attack and passed away a couple of months before the opening of his restaurant. I was not home that evening when Mom and Dad had dinner. I got the phone call that no one would like to receive when Mom told me Dad passed out at the dinner table and said someone had called 911. I rushed to the house and saw the medics were performing CPR on him. After they gave him a couple of electric shocks, they took him out to the waiting ambulance. I jumped in the car and followed it to the hospital. The view of the back of the ambulance with flashing lights is still fresh in my mind; I purposely avoid following an ambulance to this day. Mom and every one of us waited outside the operating room under the fluorescent light in the hospital. The surgeon came out and delivered the worst news of my life: they couldn't save him! I broke down and cried and couldn't believe what had just happened; it was the darkest day of my life, and it was difficult for me to go through the funeral process. I cried secretly for many years whenever I thought of Dad.

Everyone in the family was devastated and in no mood to operate the soon to be opened restaurant. The sadness of losing Dad overshadowed the grand opening of our restaurant. It was difficult to see Mom dragging herself to work as the cook at the restaurant everyday, but we had no choice because of the lack of money to hire someone else. The once hopeful investment turned into a burden for our family.

Dad was such a strong survivor and had been in good health. His untimely death was a total shock to everyone in the family. He worked hard his entire life to provide for a big family and ensured we all got a good education for a better life. Most rewarding for him was the fact that we all had the chance to attend college; his children became engineers, an MBA, a CPA, a bank manager, insurance professionals, and restaurant owners. I was overcome with sorrow, but I knew I had to be strong and carry on. I still could not believe that Dad had left us; I miss him to this day. I tried to convince myself that Dad succeeded in taking care of his family and his goal of providing us with a safe and happy home was finally realized with everyone together in the U.S., so it was time for him to rest. He was my inspiration and my hero. I could never repay what he had done for me.

I quit my part-time job with Target so I could focus on running the restaurant. When I got off work from my permanent job with Aetna Life and Casualty Company, I headed straight to the restaurant and stayed until closing at 10:00 p.m. during the week, and cleaned up for opening the following morning. I worked as much as I could on weekends and tried to spend time with Yen and Steven whenever I could. I remember emptying the grease trap over the weekend and carrying those buckets of grease to the recycling center so we could save money instead of hiring someone to do the job. It was a backbreaking work.

Nora helped run the restaurant during the day and I took over after work. Mom and Nora worked the dayshift; David, Ken and Bill took turns cooking at night while I manned the front counter and served our customers. We barely broke even because of the slowdown of the economy during the early 1980's. Christmas seasons were often busy and summer traffic also helped make up for the slower months. Despite working long hours, loan payments and high rent ate up all of the profits so everyone, including Mom, worked without pay for all those years while I held down my job with Aetna that provided the only income for me, Yen and Steven. Yen was frustrated with a situation that seemed to have no end in sight. The restaurant took a toll on me both mentally and physically; I lost weight and had trouble sleeping at night thinking about how to keep it afloat.

I put the restaurant up for sale through a commercial real estate broker, but we had no offers. Yen decided to take Steven to San Francisco while I tried to get rid of the resource-draining restaurant. In order to cut down on expenses, I rented a U-Haul truck for our belongings and drove to San Francisco. We made a stop in El Paso before continuing on to Northern California the next day. Yen's sister took her and Steven in and let them stay in her guest room on a temporary basis. I dropped the U-Haul off the following day and caught the morning flight back to Texas.

It was the first time they were away from me. I felt lost and depressed; life appeared meaningless. I felt sorry for dragging everyone in the family with me on this resource-draining endeavor. The struggle was quite different than those I had in Vietnam; it seemed much bleaker because it was personal and harder to endure. I had such high hopes for America. It almost caused me to waiver on those expectations but I knew the situation was temporary. After all, it was just about money. I had the confidence to overcome the hurdle because I was willing to work hard and committed to improving our lives as Dad had done for us.

With so much going on, I failed to notify my boss, Donna Pryor, of my absence for the journey to California. When I called her from the airport, she gave me an earful and said she could have fired my ass for taking off without proper notice. Although she was strict, Donna was a classy lady and treated everyone with respect and I knew she had my back. I returned to work and continued running the restaurant without a break.

In order to generate more income, I designed a dinner menu and began serving full service dinner in the evening with complimentary good Chinese tea and freshly brewed coffee. I served the customers myself and made them feel like they were dinning at an upscale restaurant. We slowly caught up with the payments and busy shopping seasons also helped make the situation a little better. When things calmed down, I rented a condo on Walnut Street between the restaurant and the Aetna office and moved Yen and Steven back to Texas just in time for Steven to start kindergarten.

During this time, Yen noticed that I had not had time to enjoy the music I enjoyed so much in Vietnam.

"Let's go shopping today," Yen said to me one weekend.

"What do you have in mind?" I was puzzled by her enthusiasm that day. "The Sanger Harris credit card we applied for was approved," she said with a smile. "Let's go to the Mall before your shift at the Great Wall." Yen bought me an entire stereo unit complete with a turntable at the Sanger Harris Department Store with the new credit card and gave me $200 cash to buy vinyl records that day. I spent the entire afternoon in a record store picking out the long forgotten albums of mine from the 1960's and the early 1970's. It was the first time I played those records since we left Vietnam. I was ecstatic! I began to restore the collection of songs I compiled when I was working for the PX in Vietnam.

When Yen got a job working the second shift with the Mostech Company of Carrollton, Texas, I had to babysit Steven so I took him to the restaurant and sat him behind the counter or at an empty table during down time. Steven was a very good boy; he spent his time drawing things without bothering me. I started to notice his artistic talent when I saw the lively drawings he was able to come up with by himself. He won quite a few awards as he grew older. His artwork was shown in exhibitions, and two of his "Ninja Turtle" figure drawings were published in the *Dallas Morning News*!

My First Business Trip

My boss, Donna, signed me up for a six-week training course in our Hartford Home Office. It was my first business trip, and it happened to be in January (1984), so the entire city of Hartford was covered with snow. Aetna owned an old motel across the street from the office where trainees from across the country paired up in rooms. It was located on Asylum Street, so they called it the Asylum Hotel, which was probably appropriate because of its run-down condition. Even though it was named after the street, it was a strange feeling for me as a former refugee from Vietnam to stay in a place called Asylum on Asylum Street!

Scott Fitzgerald and I shared a room. Scott came from our Walnut Creek office in Northern California, and he and I became good friends. One of the legs of the desk we used to study on was broken, so we kept it upright with one of the chairs in our room. Dad's advice concerning relentless pursuit of higher education was ingrained in me, so I took the courses very seriously and passed the tests and final exam with ease.

The majestic Aetna Headquarters we called Home Office occupied an entire city block on Farmington Street in Hartford. Aetna Life and Casualty Insurance Company was a symbol of strength and stability with an impeccable reputation dating back 150 years. It was quite a contrast between the Asylum hotel and the main office building that had security guards and five stories of office space fully equipped with cafeterias, a huge underground garage, as well as a medical facility for its employees. Our training room was on the third floor, and a team of well-qualified trainers conducted intensive training courses that kept us busy the entire time.

We had to take a series of tests and a final exam before a formal certificate of completion was handed out, along with a class photo, on the last day of our stay. The six-week training course in Hartford gave me a much-needed break from the hectic schedule back home.

When I got back to the office, I was assigned to handle claims that required on-site investigations, so they gave me a company car, which could be used for personal business with only a small charge for mileage driven.

I received an offer of $30,000 for the restaurant two years later from a young Chinese couple. Without hesitation, I finalized the deal within a week. We used up the entire check to pay off the bank and equipment loan from Watson. Although it was sad to see my hope of building a restaurant for Mom and Dad disappeared, it was a relief under the circumstances. There was also a sense of failure because I had never backed down from a challenge before. The restaurant was a cruel reminder of my Dad's untimely passing.

I was promoted to a supervisor position at the Aetna claim office in 1986. Since I was no longer required to conduct on-site claim investigations as a supervisor, I had to turn in my company car. I continued to use the

Sunbird until Yen rewarded me with a brand new fully loaded Cadillac El Dorado coup in 1988, which I proudly owned for 20+ years until I donated it to charity in 2012. It only had a little over 160,000 miles and the original engine was never worked on; the custom pearl white paint still looked as good as new. It was such a well-built luxury car, just like the Whitleys said to me 33 years ago.

Aetna had a satellite office in Lubbock, and our assistant claim manager, Mike Taylor, asked me to perform an annual audit of that office with him as a development opportunity for me to assume additional responsibilities in the future. Mike was a CPCU – a prestige designation for an insurance professional by the American Institute for Chartered Property Casualty Underwriters (CPCU). Achieving a CPCU designation requires completion of 10 college level courses covering all facets of insurance related matters, from claim handling to underwriting and insurance risk management and analysis. Mike told me if I wanted to move ahead, I might have to get my CPCU.

Mike and I flew Southwest Airlines on Monday the week of the audit and conducted audits in the morning and played golf in the afternoon. We then had a nice dinner before returning to the hotel.

"Hey Don, there is a gentleman's club down the road. Do you want to go there tonight or a restaurant for dinner?" Mike asked after a golf game one day.
"We can do both," I responded with enthusiasm.
When Mike shared the story with the folks in the office, the phrase "We can do both" became the office joke on me.
Mike and I held a wrap-up meeting at the end of the week with the management team of the Lubbock office in the morning and headed back to Dallas after lunch. After each year's audit, Mike would give me a $500 bonus as a reward. I enjoyed the time in Lubbock and appreciated the extra money from a rewarding trip.

I knew Mike sort of took me under his wing when he continued to take me to Lubbock every year from 1986 to 1991 until the Lubbock office was closed due to downsizing.

With Yen's job at the Mostech Company that manufactured computer chips in Carrollton, Texas, we bought our first house nearby in 1984. It was a newly built three-bedroom brick house in a new subdivision a block from Goode Elementary School, where Steven attended grades one through six.

After meeting the U.S. residency requirement, Yen and I took the citizenship naturalization exam and became U.S. Citizens on July 29th, 1988. Because Steven was underage, he also received his citizenship certificate the same day under Yen's and my citizenship status.

It was an emotional and proud moment for Yen and me when we were sworn in as Americans. My dream of becoming an American came true that day. When I was working for the PX admiring the American lifestyle, I said to myself, "Wouldn't it be magical if I have the opportunity to visit America?" The thought of becoming a US citizen was too far-fetched at the time. Who knew my fantasy would become a reality on that day! To me it was like winning the lottery of a lifetime. I did not have to worry about being sent to war or detained for something as simple as owning a business. Basic human rights were fully protected by the law of this land of freedom. It might be taken for granted by some, but I will treasure these rights and freedoms for the rest of my life and will always be thankful to this new country of mine. I am proud to be an American.

In 6th grade in 1991, Steven stayed late a few days after school every week and told us he was working on projects with his teacher. Yen and I didn't know his teacher asked him to paint a mural on the wall of the school gym until Yen came to the school to pick him up one day. We were shocked and proud to see he was interviewed by Channel 11 News and they showed the mural and Steven's paintings on TV. Yen and I went to the school the next day and took photos of that mural, which was still there when we returned to Carrollton for a visit a couple of years ago.

Mural painted by Steven at Goode Elementary School

Don Lao, CPCU

Inspired by Mike, I registered with the El Centro College of Dallas to begin taking CPCU courses three nights a week. After completing each course, I had to take a national exam held every six months for CPCU students. I started in 1989 and took two courses each year. I received college credits and a certificate of completion from El Centro College for each of the courses I completed, along with a certification from the American Institute for CPCU when I passed the national exam administered by the American Institute at University of Texas at Dallas.

I finally completed all 10 courses in 1993, and I was invited by the American Institute to attend the commencement ceremony in Baltimore on October 25th, 1993 where they presented me the diploma with the CPCU designation after my name. My career continued to advance with this insurance degree. It was another proud moment for me that was realized in part by my father's long and deeply held belief in the value of education. Getting the CPCU was a major milestone for me, but I knew I would not stop there. I continued to enroll in courses offered by my employer, including computer courses. I became so proficient in Excel and PowerPoint, I designed spreadsheets to track office progress and made impressive presentations using the technology. I was so proud to be referred to as an "expert" by my colleagues in these areas.

In order to encourage their employees to pursue this industry-wide recognized accomplishment, Aetna gave each newly designated CPCU a $2,500 cash bonus and an all-expenses-paid trip to attend the commencement ceremony. I booked a trip for Yen, Steven and myself and took a few extra days of vacation to extend the trip to include touring of Washington, D.C. and Atlantic City.

Following the ceremony, we spent two nights in Baltimore visiting the inner harbor and sampling its famous seafood, including crab cakes and clam chowder. We then took Steven to visit the White House and the well-known boardwalk of Atlantic City in New Jersey.

In light of the uncertainty of the fate of Hong-Kong after the handover by the British government in 1997, we took Steven back to Hong Kong to visit his birthplace in 1996. It was quite a contrast from being in Hong-Kong as a refugee in 1978 and visiting as a U.S. citizen 18 years later. Steven was never tired of the story I shared with him about how we spent time on the ship before we were allowed to come ashore. Revisiting the place was a little emotional for me. It reminds me of an important turning point of my life from fleeing Vietnam to gain freedom and reunite with my family. Hong-Kong will forever hold a special place in my heart.

After graduating from high school, Steven chose Texas Tech University in Lubbock. We were happy with his decision because I was familiar with Lubbock through my business trips and heard a lot of good things about Texas Tech from my colleagues.

AETNA-TRAVELERS MERGER

As a result of the declining economy, Aetna had been losing money and was looking for a buyer to streamline their business.

Travelers Insurance Company, a fierce competitor, bought Aetna's Property and Casualty Division in 1995 and began integrating the two companies shortly thereafter. Along with other Aetna employees of their Property and Casualty Division, I became an employee of the Travelers Insurance Company.

There was an opening in Nashville when the manager of that office retired. My boss at the Travelers office in Dallas asked if I was interested, so I sent in my resume to the hiring Regional Manager, Lynn Williams, of the Southern Region. I was told that there were a total of 33 applicants, but Lynn narrowed it down to a short list of 10 finalists and I was one of them. Lynn scheduled interviews with the final five candidates and came to Dallas to interview me. Lynn called me in March of 1997 and offered me the job to manage the Nashville Claim Office. I was very proud of winning this job while competing with so many qualified candidates. It proved to me again that Dad was right about the value of education; it is a form of wealth that can never be taken away. It also confirmed my belief in America, the land of opportunities. The working class in Vietnam would never be free from financial struggle, but people live well in America working for a good company.

I discussed the relocation offer with Yen, and she agreed to accept the offer as we would be empty nesters anyway with Steven going to Texas Tech that summer. Yen knew that I had set a goal to become a claim office manager and this would be the great opportunity to realize my dream. In addition to my experience in management, I had been reading books and articles on how to be a good manager. It was another opportunity for me to learn more about management and adopt a style that I would be comfortable with. As Dad said on many occasions, education could take any form and any setting. I could learn from running an office and managing the staff.

Nashville, Tennessee

Lynn flew Yen and me to Nashville for a visit before we officially accepted the offer to relocate. We felt good about this city of 800,000 at the time. Nashville is a beautiful city with trees and hills and a mild climate with four distinct seasons. People here are very friendly and laidback; traffic was far better than the worsening congestion in Dallas. Nashville's climate and terrain are similar to Da-Rang, Vietnam, where I spent a few years when Dad was working for the Japanese company building the hydropower plant. It was a good time to make the move so I decided to take the job.

Yen gave notice to her employer with an agreement to work until Steven moved to Lubbock in August. We put the house on the market and scheduled the mover to pack our stuff for the move.

"Don, is it okay for you to start in April?" Lynn called and asked.

"Not a problem for me but let me talk to Yen and call you back." I quickly responded.

"Lynn called and wanted me to start in April. Is it okay for you to stay here with Steven?" I asked Yen
"Sure. You'll be able to come back on the weekends, right?"
"Absolutely."
With the green light from Yen, I headed to Nashville by myself to take over management of the office in April of 1997.

Lynn scheduled an all-employee meeting to introduce me to the staff. The office was on the second floor of a four-story building in a business complex in the Metro Center of Nashville. I could see the skyline of downtown Nashville from my office window. We had a staff of 75 employees; they were a little surprised to see an Asian as their new boss as there were not many Asians living in Nashville. I shared my background and my philosophy with them and assured them of a smooth transition. They were very receptive and expressed their warm welcome. I was a little nervous taking on my first big job in America but I had been gearing up for such a position for a while, so I was well prepared for the challenge. Managing an office was quite different from managing staff of a company we owned in Vietnam; I had hired them and paid them with my own money. A manager here is also an employee, so I had to have leadership skills and savvy business knowledge in order to be successful.

After sending Steven to college, Yen joined me in Nashville. We rented an apartment while waiting for our new home to be built in Goodlettsville, Tennessee. We moved into this two-story, three-bedroom house in March of 1998.

Shortly after my arrival, Travelers Insurance Company was undergoing a transformation to enhance serving our customers with consolidated claim centers across the country. Nashville was selected as the Claim Service Center location for Tennessee and Mississippi. The Nashville office I was hired to run had only half of Tennessee as our service territory with an office in Memphis that handled the other half.

With Lynn's arrangement behind the scenes, I was interviewed by the newly appointed regional vice president for the Southeast region, who had oversight of four claim service centers – In addition to the Nashville Claim Center, the Atlanta Claim Center handled Georgia and Alabama; the Florida Claim Center handled our business in the state of Florida; and the Charlotte Claim Center had North and South Carolina as their servicing territory.

After an extensive interview in Atlanta, the senior management team offered to promote me to become the Claim Service Manager of Tennessee, overseeing the entire claim department for Tennessee and Mississippi; I had control over four offices – Nashville, Memphis, Knoxville, and Jackson, Mississippi.

When I was with Aetna Life & Casualty Insurance Company, the head of our claim department was Charlie Johnson. I admired his ability and knowledge and I set a personal goal to be a Charlie Johnson someday. I became a Charlie Johnson of Tennessee and Mississippi with the promotion – I had finally reached the pinnacle of my career!

At age 25 in Vietnam, I felt like I was on top of the world when I was holding a high-paying job with the history-making ICCS and running our family trucking company. I had the same proud feeling of accomplishment when I reached my career goal as the head of a claim service center at the Travelers Insurance Company, overseeing four offices in Tennessee and Mississippi.

Chapter 10

An Immigrant in Paradise

After 32 and half years of service with Aetna/Travelers, I announced my retirement in December of 2011, with March 30th, 2012 as my last workday. My boss threw a retirement party for me when I was in Hartford, Connecticut for a meeting. He praised and thanked me for assisting in building a better Travelers. Congratulatory emails and kind words flooded my laptop for two consecutive months.

My former assistant manager, Beth Mansfield, was promoted to become the manager of our Nashville Claim Center. Beth had been a great help to me since my move to Nashville and we became friends on a personal level. She has treated me with great respect all these years and speaks well of me whenever she has a chance, and she always shares with people that "Don hired me".

Beth put together another retirement party for me during my last week with the company in Nashville. She was in tears when she spoke to all the employees attending the party about the opportunity I gave her when the claim center was built 15 years ago. Many employees that worked with me since then also expressed their gratitude and well wishes.

In America you don't have to be rich. If you have a good job and work hard, fulfilling your dreams is almost guaranteed. Because Yen and I love to travel, she planned an eight-week European vacation to celebrate my retirement. We flew to Amsterdam on April 25th, 2012 and visited Keukenhof Garden during their annual tulip festival as our first stop. We traveled by train to Zurich, Vienna, Venice, Milan, Pisa and Rome before boarding our cruise ship that took us along the coastline of Europe from Italy to the Baltic Sea, stopping at nine other countries.

When I was in Vietnam, I read about the tulip festival of Holland, the leaning tower of Pisa, the Berlin Wall, the city that floats on water (Venice), the Coliseum of Rome, The Vatican City, the Eiffel Tower of Paris, and the London Bridge. I would not even dare to dream that I could be visiting all of these sites in person one day.

The icing on the cake was the business trips I had when I was with the Aetna and Travelers Insurance Company, which took me to 40 states, affording me the opportunity to experience the natural beauty of each of these unique states in America. The dream of seeing America when I was working for the PX in Vietnam was realized in a big way!

I told Yen on many occasions that I was a very lucky person. I was fortunate to have a Dad with the foresight and determination to give his children the best education possible. I was blessed with great parents, a loving wife, a talented son of whom I am so proud, the respect of a group of brothers and sisters who also care for one another, and I have a great relationship with Yen's family. Throughout my life I had great bosses, great friends, and great jobs. I had been lucky to have caring managers like Donna Pryor, Mike Taylor, and Lynn Williams who took me under their wings to mentor me and helped me excel. This is a life worth living!

As a way to give back, I have been actively participating in charitable activities and donations to various good causes through my employer as well as my community. When I was the manager of Travelers' Tennessee claim center, I worked diligently with our company charity foundation and obtained over $125,000 for charitable organizations in Tennessee and Mississippi. Yen and I also make donations frequently to the local

Goodwill and homeless centers. Yen has been doing volunteer work since we moved to Tennessee, and I just joined the VITA (Volunteer for Income Tax Assistance) program working with a group of volunteers at an IRS sponsored VITA site in Nashville to prepare tax returns for low-income families for free.

A refugee is often defined as an unwanted person with no nationality and thought to be a burden on the community. It is also true that many refugees have contributed richly to their adopted countries.

My family was from Guangdong, China, but I was born in Vietnam just across from the border. Therefore, the Vietnamese treated me as a foreigner, but I do not have Chinese nationality. Being an American citizen, I can proudly say I finally have a country that I truly belong to and can call my own. I am proud to be a productive citizen contributing to this great country through my jobs and paying taxes since day one of my arrival. It is a privilege to be a citizen of this great country where I can pursue my dream and enjoy the freedom that people from many places can only dream of. I am forever thankful to this new country of mine.

The winding path of my life has been filled with ups and downs, I learned to forget the difficult times and continue to forge ahead to better myself and provide for the ones that I love. My goal is to live a meaningful and productive life.

My family is not rich, but we have a great life in the U.S., living in nice houses, owning nice cars, and visiting many great places. Being able to enjoy my retirement in this wonderful country, I am truly an immigrant in paradise!

Acknowledgement

I would like to dedicate this book to my Dad who had devoted his entire life caring for his family and who provided me with the highest education possible. He rescued me from near death when I was sent to combat while I was with the 5th Airborne Division. I owe everything to this hero of mine.

My gratitude goes to our sponsor, Mr. and Mrs. Whitley who brought our family from the refugee camp in Fort Smith, Arkansas, to Texas. They provided our family with housing and patiently helped us get acclimated to the new life in America and took care of our needs. They provided my Dad and David with jobs so our family was able to be self-sufficient and back on our feet in a short period of time.

I would like to thank Mr. Si for the friendship and for taking care of Yen and me when we were refugees in Hong-Kong, as well as for his support and guidance in rebuilding our trucking company in Vietnam.

I would like to thank Lieutenant Roger Story for sharing his personal roadside-bomb experience with us.

I would like to give special thanks to Donna Pryor, my former boss and our best friend, who took me under her wing and mentored me so skillfully. Her guidance was a major factor that led to my success as a claims professional in the Insurance industry.

I would like to thank my former colleague, Mike Taylor, for inspiring me to become a CPCU when I was with the Aetna Life and Casualty Company.

To Lynn Williams, the Regional Vice President with the Travelers Company who gave me the opportunity to manage the Nashville claim office and subsequently become the Tennessee Claim Service Manager. Without Lynn's belief in me, I would not have been able to reach the pinnacle of my career.

To my Mom for her love and for her care and support at every stage of my life.

To my brothers and sisters for the love and support throughout my life.

To my talented son, Steven, for his love and for his encouragement and support as I wrote this book. I am so proud of him.

To my loving wife, Yen, for her love and support all these years. Without her love and support, I would not be who I am today. I love her more than anything else.

$\mathcal{S}$ources

In completing this book, I drew upon related materials from the following two books:

1. The Book "**Boat People**".
2. The Chinese Book "**History of Vietnamese Chinese**" by Mr. Lieu Nguyen of Los Angles, CA. Book ID – ISBN 1-890474-07-X.

www.ingramcontent.com/pod-product-compliance
Lightning Source LLC
Chambersburg PA
CBHW022255290526
45785CB00015B/1009